DECEPTION
REVELATION TO RELEASE

*Response to my secret
Christian gay spouse*

Deborah Nottingham

ISBN 978-1-64471-748-6 (Paperback)
ISBN 978-1-64471-749-3 (Digital)

Covenant Books, Inc.
11661 Hwy 707
Murrells Inlet, SC 29576
www.covenantbooks.com

For my parents:
Jerry and Venita Nottingham,
inherently godly, supportive and loving parents
who have been married over 60 years.

Keep deception and lies far from me,
Give me neither poverty nor riches;
Feed me with the food that is my portion,
That I not be full and deny You and say,
"Who is the Lord?"
Or that I not be in want and steal,
And profane the name of my God

—Proverbs 30:8 (NASB)

CONTENTS

CHAPTER 1

BETRAYAL: THE FIRST THREE DAYS

I did not know when I left that Friday morning that I would never sit down with my husband of twelve years again. I saw him twice more, and the second time, I had a gun with me. I left our Texas townhouse sweating in my conservative summer suit and threw my briefcase in the Toyota. I have no memories of unusual arguments. If we had made love recently, I have no memory of it. Things were not bad. Not good. Just another day, I thought.

Daily devotions were my habit, and I am sure I spoke to God that morning, probably before I spoke to my husband. Tom worked evenings in his startup dental practice and usually was still in bed when I left. I worked for the hospital, and I loved working with physicians and helping cancer patients. Meetings, lunch, reports, and calls were all part of that routine Friday.

My phone rang at the end of the workday. Our marriage counselor said, "I have some difficult news for you. You need to be tested for HIV and AIDS."

Silence.

"What?"

"You need to be tested for HIV and AIDS."

"Does this mean my husband is gay?" I replied when I could speak.

"Maybe or maybe not. I can't say, but you need to be tested for your own safety," the counselor answered.

Sitting at my desk with the phone to my ear, looking out my window at the medical complex toward the blazing sun, I was stunned. I felt overwhelmed. I could not breathe. Fuzzy fragile feelings separated my mind from my body. Alone in my office. Thank God.

My friend, Renae, worked in the same hospital.

I called her and said, "You were right. I am not going home. I need to be tested for HIV/AIDS, and I need help."

Renae had asked me on the racquetball court two weeks earlier, "Do you think your husband is gay?" I missed that next shot. No one had ever verbalized this thought to me in my twelve years of marriage. Not friends, not family, not even myself.

"I don't think so, but I have wondered about some weird things," I replied.

I was too distraught to drive, so Renae took me to the ATM to withdraw the maximum allowable amount of money from our account. We drove to her gated apartment complex and went inside to her apartment.

"Now we need food," she said and fixed something to eat—her favorite comfort food, spaghetti shells, a can of tomatoes, and a half stick of butter.

I wept. I didn't think I could eat, but I did swallow. She cleaned up dishes while I sat frozen at the table. She told me to take a shower, gave me some pajamas, and made me a bed on the couch. It was the first night of my new life. Someone was taking care of me. I was a robot, but at least I was not alone. I did not call my husband or speak to him for two days, and I did not care if he was frantic with worry. It was the first time in over a decade I took care of my feelings and myself first. This new behavior required the support of a willing friend.

Saturday, we picked up my car from work and went to the bank again. I pulled out fifty percent of our joint savings and opened a new account in my name. I was terrified at the bank and kept looking around furtively. I was thinking I could not do this to him. He would come into the bank and find me. There had to be an explanation. This couldn't be happening. God, why is this happening? Irrational emotions erupted to the surface.

We went by the house to pick up some clothes for me. I knew my husband would be working on Saturday morning, and once we drove by his office and saw his car there, I felt safe enough to go home, at least for a few minutes. My heart thumped and then throbbed with pain as I entered the townhouse. I grabbed enough clothes for one week of work and exercise and ran out the door. Renae kept watch for his return.

When I reached the door to leave, I turned back to get the one thing that I treasured most: a collage of pictures of my parents, four sets of grandparents, and my six great-grandparents taken with me as a baby. I locked the door behind me and left the things that defined what I had known as my life with Tom.

Sunday, I called Tom and told him what the counselor had said. I had written down what I wanted to say. It was a short conversation. He yelled about how worried he was about me. He was furious with me and with the counselor and said he would sue him for breach of confidence. I would not tell my husband where I was, just that I was alive. I had to think about every word I would communicate to him and to others.

After we spoke, I called my parents and told them what had happened on Friday. My mother started to cry. My father asked me, "Are you sure? Do you have to leave him?"

I remember shouting at my dad, "Do you want me to die? I may have HIV or AIDS from him. If I do not have it and go back to him, then I might get it."

Mom came on and said, "What do you need from us? Where are you? Are you safe?"

I assured her that I was all right for now, that I had some money and some clothes and was with Renae. I gave them her phone number and told them to call me at work if they needed to contact me.

Sunday afternoon, Renae said I had to buy a steering wheel lock for my car. "What?" I said.

"You have to have transportation, money, and clothes to survive the next few weeks. He will try to steal your car," she informed me.

After work on Monday, she and I went to a taco restaurant for margaritas and fajitas. When we came out of the restaurant, my car was gone.

She asked me, "Did you put the steering wheel lock on the Toyota?"

"Well, no, as I had no idea that he would follow me from work. Maybe someone else stole it?" I said.

We called the police and they asked, "Are you and your husband having problems?"

It was so embarrassing to say yes. He suggested we look around the parking lot for our other older car, and there it was. I was shocked. Tom had stolen my car.

Renae is Louise to my Thelma from the old movie Thelma and Louise. She said, "He will not get away with this. Come on, let's go find the car."

We drove to the house, but my car was not there. "He will not think you would do this, so let's drive the blocks nearby."

Sure enough, we found my stolen car—with the steering wheel lock on the floorboard, as Tom did not have the key to put it on the wheel. We parked the old car behind the Toyota, jumped in and drove off. I have never before done anything so crazy or exhilarating in my life, and I laughed until I wet my pants. I could only imagine his surprise the next morning. Then fear kicked in. What will be his next retaliation? I had that car for two more years, but the potential ramifications to my defiance were terrifying.

During this time, I clung to the scripture John 15:16 (NAS): "You did not choose Me, but I chose you, and appointed you, that you should go and bear fruit, and that your fruit should remain, that whatever you ask of the Father in My name, He may give to you." I did not know exactly what to ask God, but I knew I could not deny the issues or trust my husband again. Now what?

I was scared. Often. Words spoken in a verbally harmful way are so destructive that the victim prefers silence, and that is where you withdraw. Into silence. You hold yourself tightly against the wounds, and spoken wounds, unlike physical wounds, are not evident on the outside. Anyone who has ever lived with a cruel or even abusive person can attest to the fact that most of their time is spent walking on eggshells. You can't predict what mood the perpetrator will be in when they come home or what will set him off in a rage. You spend your time performing, either to access their snippets of niceness or to show the world, especially your Christian friends, that everything is all right.

Some people understand your challenges and will ask you (and mean it), "How are you, really?" But most people do not want to be involved. Your true friends do want to know and will be there for you, even if you are too afraid to speak. When I finally conquered enough of my fear to act, they were the ones who found me a safe place to be, encouraged me to take action to protect myself, advised me to protect my children and pets (even though I did not have either), and to take care of my finances. They will keep the cat or dog, go to the bank with you to withdraw enough cash to survive, help you to flee, look for your car that the abuser stole from the parking lot, and stand with you and the police when you make your report.

I believe God brings godly people "with skin on" to stand beside us in the darkest night. Renae was a Christ-follower friend who helped me to leave my abusive marriage. It was Renae who confronted me on the racquetball court about my husband's sexual orientation. The idea that he might have fallen in love with another guy occurred to me when we lived overseas three years before. He was crazy about this man, wanted to spend time with him, and was dismissive of me when his friend was around. But my husband and I had left Switzerland to start again in the States, and I thought that was the end of it. How wrong I was.

> Deception: The act of causing someone to accept
> as true or valid what is false or invalid: the act of
> deceiving. (Merriam Webster Dictionary)

> Deceive: To cause to believe what is untrue.
> (Merriam Webster Dictionary)

Other words are used for deception: betrayal, duplicity, trickery, cheat, dirt, fraudulent, insincerity, and pretense. All of these words describe an aspect of my life with a man who struggled with same-sex attraction while married to a woman. His pretense of attraction to me was so deep that I did not detect anything for almost a decade.

Was he a fraud? A fake? I truly believe we were best friends and loved one another. We had each waited many years to find "the one" and were very matched in interests and intelligence. Where we failed personally and in our relationship was in speaking truth. Truth sets you free, and we lived a lie for thirteen years.

The core issue of my anger and depression was not my spouse's sexuality but his deception. I ask in my journal, months later, "Why did you marry me and keep me in the marriage relationship for so long? More importantly, why did I not know all this was not normal and I needed to get out?" Deception for us was living the lie of marital harmony. Deception for him was duplicity of his true identity. Deception for me was a denial of relational needs, fraudulent living, and tolerating normal but unmet expectations. Deception is not uncommon, and there are many reasons for deception between romantic partners.

Deception and our desire to deceive come from our human nature. As a Christ follower who studies the Bible, I recognize the Evil One, the great deceiver. The first book of the Bible tells the story of the fall from God's favor when the serpent says to the woman, "Has God said? And you surely will not die!" and she believes him and eats the fruit. Jesus says, in John 8:44 (NIV), "You are of your father the devil, and you want to do the desires of your father. He was a murderer from the beginning and does not stand in the truth because there is no truth in him. Whenever he speaks a lie, he speaks from his own nature, for he is a liar and the father of lies." At the end of the Bible in Revelation 12:9 (NIV), John says, "And the great dragon was thrown down, the serpent of old who is called the devil and Satan, who deceives the whole world; he was thrown down to the earth, and his angels were thrown down with him."

Deception. This is the issue that almost destroyed my life.

The Bible also tells us stories of man-to-man deceit. Cain said to God, "Am I my brother's keeper?" after he murdered his brother Abel. Abraham had his wife lie to the king and say she was his sister, and then the king slept with her. Jacob deceived his father and pretended to be his brother Esau, by putting skins on his arms. Joseph's brothers lied to their father and told him Joseph was killed. The brothers killed a goat and dipped Joseph's coat in blood to convince their father. King David's son, Ammon, pretended to be ill on his bed so he could lure and rape his sister. King Herod tried to deceive the wise men seeking baby Jesus into revealing his location so he could kill the baby Jesus.

Even if you are not a Christ follower, history shows many examples of deception between men. Governments, military commanders, companies, religious leaders, sports leaders, and politicians have all deceived men. The U.S. Government experimented on black citizens in Alabama by promising them free healthcare and giving them syphilis to see the effects. Quaker Oats and MIT gave radioactive cereal to retarded children in the 1940s without their parents' knowledge or consent. (Source: https://www.nytimes.com/.../settlement-reached-in-suit-over-radioactive-oatmeal-experi…January 1, 1998)

The successful D-Day invasion of Normandy relied on a deliberate deception of Hitler, through radio, messages, and spies, to keep the location of the invasion secret. Throughout the Middle Ages, disagreement with religious leaders could result in a label of heretic and even execution, so people were forced into deception and pretending. Hitler and Stalin lied to their people about their intentions. American presidents are known for their "deceptive politics." Think of doping scandals and the elaborate schemes to achieve success in sports that occur today.

Literature depicts deception as well. Shakespeare in *Romeo and Juliet* shows Juliet faking her death in order to avoid marrying another man. Juliet awakens to find Romeo dead from his self-inflicted wound after mourning her "death." In *A Tale of Two Cities*, Dickens gives us lawyer Sydney Carten. In *The Last Leaf*, O. Henry gives an artist who paints a leaf on a wall to keep a woman from dying, only to die himself. Homer in *The Iliad* gives us the famous Trojan horse. Spy novels are masterful recreations of deceit on a grand scale.

You have your own personal examples of deception if you ever believed in Santa Claus and the Tooth Fairy. Your friends or family have betrayed you in big and small ways. Families have hidden and covered up abuse by fear and lack of acknowledgement. This can be harmful to the survivor of abuse. Deception, thankfully, is almost always unmasked over time. We are hopeful that we will survive the deception, and healing will occur as truth is revealed. Healing happens with hard work and the ability to face reality. But trusting people again—well, that takes a long time.

Their throat is an open grave, with their tongues they keep deceiving, The poison of asps is under their lips. (Romans 3:13, NASB)

If we say that we have no sin, we are deceiving ourselves and the truth is not in us. (1 John 1:8, NASB)

CHAPTER 2
FALSEHOOD: THE FIRST WEEK

What I remembered when I left the counselor's office after he confirmed to my face that I needed to have an HIV/AIDS blood test was the verse in the Bible from James about trials. I passed my husband on my way into the counselor's office, and his anger shimmered around him like a gossamer cloud. He pushed against me as we passed. I had been re-reading an old journal and was saddened by the fact that I have been unhappy, scared, and angry with my husband for at least three years. Events change, but the issues remained. I had buried myself trying to keep the peace. I did not feel the "joy through trials." My anger at him was so big it was bound to explode in a messy and deliberately unholy way very soon.

Journal

August 1, 1992

Consider it pure joy, my brothers, whenever you face trials of many kinds, because you know that the testing of your faith develops perseverance. Perseverance must finish its work so that you may be mature and complete, not lacking anything. (James 1:2–4, NIV)

I am angry but have not yet expressed it for fear of what? The counselor wants me to use this time to vent emotionally, but I cannot go there.

My neck is tight and my breathing is controlled. I have laid here in fear of starting this process of "working" on myself and on the relationship.

Why do I have to move out before he will seek help? My husband has locked the door and changed the lock and demanded money that was ours together is given back to him. Like hell! I took half of it, if we are married through the end of the year; we are both responsible for the taxes, so I keep it. I am furious at him, because this process of therapy is for him. I think he is very ill, and I am on the periphery. I have moved into depression and do not want to leave and go into the real world. I have old underwear, and that infuriates me. I want this separation process to be completed and have my things around me.

The silence of being alone in an apartment is frightening but refreshing. To think that in three weeks I will face this silence daily for months, maybe years, fills me with anticipation. I will buy a house and a dog when I return from vacation. I need this time in the mountains alone. I will have just moved in to the new apartment for two weeks before I leave. I must make some plans for what I will do in Idaho.

I had a dream about sharing my office at the hospital with someone and was ranting up and down the street with my high school friends. I still cannot direct my anger at him, because it is so big. I am in this anger process as my biological clock ticks off.

My vision: a happy marriage with someone and some step-kids. I do not hold up hope for change, and without change I do not stay. Eleven and a half years are enough. I cannot even touch the verbal abuse, homosexuality, alcohol use, anger, and hate for family issues yet. Do you go for the throat or for the issues you may not get consensus on?

I will start to see my own therapist this week, not our joint marriage counselor, and keep Jim as marital therapy if my husband agrees. I don't like men now, and I have doubts about Jim, our mutual counselor, "protecting" me versus "using" me to help his ill patient. He backs away from issues of hospitalization and homosexuality to keep therapy going.

What are the things I most want to change about myself?

1. Stop needing everyone to "like" me.
2. Decrease anxiety about money and being alone.
3. Develop sensitivity to other people's feelings about issues I see as black and white.
4. Handle anger assertively and effectively.
5. Deal with conflict and difficult situations without worry and procrastination.

My counseling work showed me these were my anger producing events:

1. My husband demanding "his" money back.
2. Locking me out of my house.
3. Causing fear from his anger.
4. People not doing their job.
5. Person changing 180 degrees on issues.
6. Anxiety over past meetings makes me fearful for the next meeting.

My Lies

1. *I must have everyone's love and approval.* "Am I now trying to win the approval of men, or of God? Or am I trying to please men? If I were still trying to please men, I would not be a servant of Christ" (Galatians 1:10, NIV).
2. *It is easier to avoid problems than to face them.* "Brothers, I do not consider myself yet to have taken hold of it. But one thing I do: Forgetting what is behind and straining toward what is ahead, I press on toward the goal to win the prize for which God has called me heavenward in Christ Jesus" (Philippians 3:13–14, NIV).
3. *I cannot be happy unless things go my way.* "I am not saying this because I am in need, for I have learned to be content whatever the circumstances. I know what it is to be in need, and I know what it is to have plenty. I have learned the secret of being content in any and every situation, whether well fed or hungry, whether living in plenty or in want. I can do everything through Him who gives me strength" (Philippians 4:11–13, NIV).

Marital Lies:

1. *It is his entire fault.* "You, therefore, have no excuse, you who pass judgment on someone else, for at whatever point you judge the other, you are condemning yourself, because you who pass judgment do the same things. Now we know that God's judgment against those who do such things is based on truth. So when you, a mere man, pass judgment

on them and yet do the same things, do you think you will escape God's judgment?" (Romans 2:1–3, NIV).

2. *You owe me.* "Young men, in the same way be submissive to those who are older. All of you, clothe yourselves with humility toward one another, because, 'God opposes the proud but gives grace to the humble." Humble yourselves, therefore, under God's mighty hand, that he may lift you up in due time. Cast all your anxiety on him because he cares for you." (1 Peter 5:5–7).

Journal

August 2, 1992

What happened to my husband? Why am I drawn to needy people? My sorrow is beyond healing! My heart is faint within me. "Heal me, O Lord, and I will be healed; save me and I will be saved, for you are the one I praise" (Jeremiah 17:14, NIV).

My father and his father were mean verbally—I loved them, my dad and my husband, and put up with it. My realization of a family pattern of verbal abuse started with a family diagram I created with my counselor and the inter-connectedness of family. We also looked at my husband's mother's breakdown. Who gave spiritual leadership in the family? The women. Every part of the family has an under-functioning male. The grandfather was mean physically to his kids. My husband's dad was not the spiritual leader, and he had huge unresolved conflicts with his father.

I have told the counselor about my mental illness between ages 14–19 with descriptions of the porch discussion with my mom's sister where she asked me to choose whom to live with when my parents divorced. The voices I heard in my head were of a man yelling for me to choose which voice of my father's mother, or my mother I would listen to. In the mental breakdowns, I always had to choose between my mother and my father's mother's rescue. I have not spoken of this to anyone, and it will be several years before I can understand the significance of these stories. I flash back to these details I told the therapist.

I had my first break with reality on my front porch when I was fourteen. My mother's sister told me that if my parents broke up, I would go with her and live with her parents. Why did this fill me with such terror at the age of fourteen? For the five years they occurred, I never discussed the voices that were continuously in my head. I dreamed I was at the gate of a concentration camp with my father's mother and my mother inside. I must choose who will be saved, and the anxiety of this decision makes me lose touch with reality. My father's mother was my mentor and my favorite supportive family member. My mother I loved deeply, but we pulled away from each other in my adolescence, especially after her hysterectomy at age thirty-two, with all her ensuing craziness. I did not understand the significance of the dream until much later.

The thoughts of the righteous are just, but the counsels of the wicked are deceitful. (Proverbs 12:5, NASB)

CHAPTER 3
TREACHERY:
REACTIONS OF FRIENDS

Call in the troops. Sound the alarm. Shock them with the story of unbelievable betrayal, and they will reject him and surround you with support. It does not matter what form it takes, the wounded-ness of deception and betrayal is messy. I was not godly, I was not kind, I was not loyal. I was furious. I first called my friends and those who knew us well as a couple.

The story was still shocking in the early 1990s, but our mutual couple friends had noticed the problems in the marriage. They offered their ears, their support. I left them to deal with their reactions on their own. The more outgoing wife guides the social life of many couples, and we were no exception. The wives become friends first, and the husbands follow. It is rare for both members of a couple to equally like both members of another couple. We both liked a couple in Switzerland and did many things together there. Most of my husband's dental school friends had moved away from town, so our friends in Texas were mostly people I knew from work and church. There was one exception. A couple at church really supported him during this time, and I am very thankful that they showed God's love to him. Mostly, what Tom experienced from our mutual friends was rejection.

My second volley of attack was through our church. I called the church office and said I had left my husband and needed to speak to an elder or leader. I met with an elder the next day. After praying together, I told him that I had to be tested for AIDS, and he offered to help me move out if that is what I chose to do. He also told me that he would contact my husband to see how they could support him. We had been going to a big Evangelical Church since we returned from Switzerland and were involved in a Sunday school class together. I wanted them to kick him out, break fellowship, and protect me so that I could attend church without fear. They did not do that.

Lastly, I wanted my non-Christian friends and work colleagues to know what the man had done to me. They were my best source for anger and revenge discussions. My secretary, Brenda, organized the posse that would help me move out of my home. She found the locksmith who would illegally break into the house in my husband's absence. I gave her a list of friends who were willing to help, and she helped to find two pickups for the process.

We met at 8:30 a.m. on a Saturday near where my husband lived. Mutual friends and friends from my church and from work all watched him from a safe distance in cars that he would not recognize. We saw him leave in the old car and head for the office. I had spent Friday evening mentally going through each room and tagging things I wanted to take. I had tried to get into the townhouse a week earlier, but the locks had been changed. Our locksmith friend arrived and opened the door within ten minutes. He was not comfortable doing this, but I paid him in cash, and Brenda assured him we would only take what was mine.

I walked into the house and frantically labeled things I wanted to take with yellow Post-it notes. The ladies brought in the boxes and the newspapers, and the men started loading the furniture I had marked. I was terrified that Tom would return and make a scene. I felt unbelievably sad.

Renae kept saying to me, "Keep going, it will be all right."

Things I held most precious were missing from the townhouse. My Christmas ornaments and decorations, photo albums, and quilts were not there. Renae had been divorced, as had a couple of the other people with me. They said to make sure you take anything that is a pair; otherwise, what you have will feel like an "extra" piece of furniture. So I did not take our cherished Danish Modern bedroom set, just both the nightstands. My clothes were already packed, and I took a lounge chair, a side chair, and the family heirlooms. We were done in less than two hours, and we headed for my new apartment in a gated community.

I always wondered what Tom did and said when he came home that evening to an apartment that was empty of half our possessions. I had not taken much, but after I realized what he had hidden away, I did not want to lose anything else. I picture him screaming, kicking things, and cursing me for hours. It was a final torrent of blows to the enemy.

Journal

August 10, 1992

How do I recall the last eight days? My head is spinning with all my freedoms, happiness, and joy. I finally got all my stuff last week in one-and-a-half hours with help from my friends. My friends were doing whatever was needed. We hired a locksmith to break-in to my own apartment. My husband had hidden my Christmas things, which were so precious to me. My clothes were packed and my photo albums were also gone. They were not in the apartment. I took my family dining room table, chairs, buffet and china cabinet, and all my china from my grandparents. I had a futon to sleep on, two chairs from the living room, two nightstands, and the kitchen utensils.

After I moved everything out, Renae and I went to a friend's lake house north of Austin. The moonlight and water was exquisite and I enjoyed the friendship and had too much sun. A jet ski goes past the lake house, makes a complete circle, and goes away quickly fading out of sight. Lord, what are you telling me in the waves? When the turn is made, the waves at the apex calm quickly. But where the waves interact, there is roughness as the new and old waves collide in intersecting waves. Then the path clears as they move in less frequently intersecting ripples.

The next few months are going to be tough as I rethink new ways, thoughts, and actions. I am so happy. I feel like a balloon with the string letting go—floating free.

After physically hiding from him, scared, and realizing how sick he is, I must get out of the relationship! Therapy was so bad that day before I was told I needed to get tested for HIV. He was angry, and the therapist allowed it. No more joint sessions. My individual meeting with the therapist Nancy was great. She was affirming of me and said my husband was ill and that the therapist cannot use me to help his patient get better. "Praise God that it is not your job to fix your husband. That is God's job." She is right.

My best friend told me a story about a man on a bridge with rope. He gives the rope to another man to hold and ties it around himself and jumps off the bridge. He keeps demanding that the guy at the top "save" him, but the man who jumped will not do anything to help himself. Finally, the man on the bridge cannot hold on any longer and lets go of the rope. Even if the man tells the guy on the bridge that he must save him, he cannot save him alone.

Abuse is a common theme in discussion today: emotional, sexual, physical, or spiritual. During my marriage, I realized I had experienced some of those things at various degrees. And yet, I still felt the failure of our marriage was my fault. I was not pretty enough. Good enough. Nice enough. If I was a better wife, woman, or Christian, I could save him from destroying us and the marriage. Abuse has wounds that can be seen and those that are hidden. Friends that come to our aid in crisis and do things with us and for us are invaluable. Cultivate those friends.

O Lord, You have deceived me and I was deceived; You have overcome me and prevailed. I have become a laughingstock all day long; everyone mocks me. (Jeremiah 20:7, NASB)

CHAPTER 4
UNTRUTH: REMORSE

The shock wore off, the anger was spent, and I was left with my things and myself. I moved into a one-bedroom apartment with very few things. I went to the store and bought two good single-bed mattresses to use as mattress and box springs. Surely this would all be temporary, and then I could use them for my guest room. (I still had those mattresses eighteen years later.)

Renae had moved back to Ohio from her temporary assignment at our hospital in Texas. She said, years later, that she believed she was sent to Texas to be with me during that time. She was wise, kind, and strong, and we have remained friends for all these years. Now the reality is upon me. I will probably lose my marriage, lose my position as a wife, lose my status as a Bible study leader, and my biological clock will explode. All my identity is being stripped away from me like the seeds of a dandelion in a strong wind. I did not have children. I cannot imagine what it would take to protect them, to deal with changing their environment, their pets, and their school changes as I processed my own upheaval.

Journal

August 15, 1992

It takes great courage for me to start to write now.
I have such pain in my chest, I cannot breathe.
I have cooked, watched TV, scanned books, and

31

slept—anything to avoid this deep pain. I am depressed. Renae left for her home in Ohio yesterday, and I was so sad. I cried uncontrollably, weeping in the bathroom. It was like another loss. Without her, I would be floating in a sea of misery. She has praised me for my legs, body, hair, face, personality, friendliness, and everything about my work. It is like feeding a bottomless pit of absence of positive statements. She showed her own vulnerabilities and was willing to share the pain that my pain caused her. She believes I should "cut my losses" and start again. She has encouraged my hope of new passion, love, and healing. I have enjoyed a rich fantasy life of romance the last few days.

I shared my pain with my church counselor, and he validated that he was there for me. I had value to God and a purpose in life. He also acknowledged that if I were "pursued" by my husband, as a man should love his wife, I would run to it. But until his sins and my part of the failure are dealt with, we have to be apart. What will I do when I see him again? The counselor believes my husband will drop out of all religious activities. I feel guilty because my husband will use me as "the reason" for stopping church and even therapy. But it is his choice. My therapist believes that I must go through this pain, not around it as I have done in the past. It will help me to heal quicker. I continue to see only my husband's issues, and she wants me to focus on me. A realization of a fourteen-year-old girl who is so pulled apart by her parent's emotional distance, that she became psychotic, that is me. That description devastated my image of the marriage falling apart being only his problem. I am also playing the part of the "enabler" for my husband and feel responsible for fixing others and my husband. I have asked my parents to write about the time 20 years ago when I was really crazy. I remember my parents were fighting about me, and I told them I would not let them control my life. I was trying to fix their marriage as well and saw it as all my fault and responsibility.

Emotionally I must become whole, but I am living in a romantic fantasy of being with any man that is kind to me. As I write, the pain becomes warmth as I acknowledge the pain and it is not as frightening. My therapist wants me to write a letter to my husband saying everything that I am feeling. It terrifies me.

I was always grown-up responsible, "an easy child to raise" per my father. I stayed alone all summer long from the fourth grade when I was nine years old. I would get myself to school, and have to figure out what to do if I missed the bus. I fixed my own breakfast every school day, because my mom went to work in the meatpacking factory. As a teenager, I kept the house, cooked, and worked at home to help my parents. I felt that I must perform and succeed for my parents to be proud of me.

My husband said, "He waited 28 years to find the 'love of his life'." I am being drawn back, I want to go "back" to him, forgive him and be forgiven. Since I have made such a personal statement about leaving, I don't want to disappoint all my supportive friends and myself. I will not return without change, but it does not mean I do not want to go back to my husband. The more I read about codependency, the more pain I feel.

Heartache and pain is all I feel for all the lack of emotion still un-surfaced.

It had been only a month, and my need for love and affection was a constant, nagging weight. I looked at other men after I took off my wedding ring. If someone was kind to me, my eyes glistened. I was quicksand waiting for anyone to step close and be sucked into my neediness. Having a job helped me function, at least superficially, and going to therapy gave me something to do. Lack of companionship or lists of tasks to do for my husband and the household was both freeing and terrifying. I want him back. He is my best friend, my lover, and my husband. I have just had my arm cut off, and the blood drips as my life force flows out of me. God help me, I want him back.

And through his shrewdness He will cause deceit to succeed by his influence; and he will magnify himself in his heart, and he will destroy many while they are at ease. (Daniel 8:25, NASB)

CHAPTER 5
CUNNING: REQUIREMENTS

It is important to talk during a separation process. I never spoke with my husband after the Friday I found out I needed to be tested for HIV/AIDS except once, on the phone, two days later. Not for days. Not for months. There were no words between us, only hateful, dismissive, and angry actions. I regret my inability to confront and begin to heal with Tom. There is a gaping wound of unresolved issues that I still feel decades later.

In a therapy session, I discussed some of the behaviors I had seen in the last four months of our marriage. I described a time when I had gone to bed first, as I almost always did. When Tom came to bed, he would wrap around me until he fell asleep. It sounds sweet and cuddly, but if I moved before he moved away in sleep, he would wake up and be angry. He would jump out of bed, scream at me to lay still, scare me to death, and go somewhere else to sleep. One particular night, I remembered I could not go back to sleep. I crept out of bed and walked to the other bedroom, but he was not there. I went quietly down the stairs and heard a strange noise, like a brush going rapidly over a hard surface. When I got to the kitchen, he was on his hands and knees with a toothbrush going over the grout at two o'clock in the morning.

"What are you doing?" I asked quietly.

"I have to get it clean," he replied. He just kept scrubbing. I went back to bed.

Tom was bizarre. No wonder I was crazy as well.

Journal

August 18, 1992

Letter to my husband during our separation, written at the request of my therapist.

What are you doing now? Are you on the telephone, out having a drink, reading, exercising, anything but the hard work of change? It is so painful, but the anger I feel covers over the pain. I have tested the waters of aloneness and have had little personal contact with people outside of work on a few occasions. What I feel is the joy, peace, freedom, and happiness of being away from your craziness!

The habits of the past eleven years grate on me, and I also have my laundry list of remembrances: (a) anger and judgment, (b) critical spirit, (c) no spiritual life, (d) drinking with subsequent change in your personality, (e) vanity of personal appearance, (f) cleanliness over messiness, (g) no friendships of your own, (h) obsessed with work, (i) horrible relationship with your family, (j) rejection of me sexually, (k) never satisfied with your life, (l) need for stimulation and entertainment constantly, (m) unavailable for emotional support.

What is so odd is that I have not seen you for almost four weeks after being together almost daily for thirteen years, and I have no regrets. I remember wanting to see you this weekend, missing you, and thinking about stopping this painful process of rebuilding. I know our lives are irrevocably intertwined, because I am looking at everything in a new way. Is it OK for me to eat chips and guacamole? What if I want to sleep naked? How cool should I keep the apartment? What if I skip a week of exercise? Are my thighs all right with some padding? Am I really pretty? Is my ability to "get things done efficiently" wrong, or is it useful? Is it all right to not do something at home? Can I have a glass of wine in the evening? If I spend time with my friends after work, why do you consider that wrong and fill me with guilt when I come home? Do I have to wait my entire life for a dog? Why have I never gone to a dog show? Why does my every activity outside of work have to meet with your approval and my mental checklist? I am just as crazy as you.

I am so angry with you for using God and religion to try to "keep me in line" and for not meeting my needs, because you are the man and must be free to do whatever you want. This is control at its most religious; I just did not have a name for it then.

Even when I went to graduate school—the race was on to complete it. You had to have more schooling than me. Competition? Even though you had three degrees, and I was perfectly content to have my Medical Technology Bachelor-degreed husband, you now wanted to be a "doctor." I just wanted you.

We fought like crazy in our first six months of marriage. I spent many nights on the stairwell of our townhouse silently crying while I watched you sleep downstairs and never understanding why you could not sleep with me. We enjoyed having our first apartment and entertaining guests. You supported me financially and emotionally. We moved to the mouse-infested apartment, because I went to graduate school and was not working full time. The mice would come out of the stove coils and look at me while I studied. The roach traps would be wiggling because of the mouse that had gone inside to eat the roaches and got stuck. I hated that place and was ashamed that we lived there.

You decided to go to dental school, even though you had already rejected going to medical school and majoring in Psychiatry. This would only take four years of training instead of seven, and the race was on. I had only eighteen months to complete my MBA before you would move for school to a new city. One semester required me to take eighteen graduate hours, and I damn near lost my mind. I completed my Masters work, but had no celebration or graduation because we were moving on to your dreams and your pursuits. Now it was up to me to support the family, and the pressure was great. I made only $1,000 per month in 1983, and we barely made the bills. I had no contacts or experience in my new city and field. You were trying to be a Christian, but the classmates rejected you, so you became mean, sarcastic, to fit in with the crowd.

We bought two chairs, a couch, and a piano for me from savings and stayed in an unsafe neighborhood where it was convenient for your school. My ten-hour days with a nutcase paled in comparison to your first year dental school trauma. I ended up after one year with a neck so stiff it would not move and ulcers at the age of twenty-seven. So you took me to a therapist you found at the University to teach me biofeedback for stress management. When this therapy occurred, I had decided I wanted to buy a house when I got my new job. The payments were affordable; we were in a good neighborhood, with a short commute and had lovely weekends. You spent the first summer you were off working on the house, and I remember being so happy to be settled.

School started again for your sophomore year, and my memories are of sharing supper and no more contact verbally until you came to bed. You would wake me up nightly and hold on to me in the spoon position and request that I not move until you went to sleep. I would get a neck cramp holding still. If I moved, you would get mad. What was that about?

The pattern continued of a family death every spring for four years and included my uncle, your grandfather, my grandmother, and nearly me.

The junior year of dental school is a missing blur of time for me, because you were at school constantly. Professionally, I was now promoted and working with a group of people I really liked. I was growing professionally and spiritually, and I was learning and growing with bible classes. I worked well with physicians and was successful. We tried to be involved as a couple with church, but you were too busy with school. Between your junior and senior year you worked in the lab at the University. You were always too busy meeting your own needs, and I never felt that the sacrifice was for our future, but that my sacrifice was for your future.

Then came the baby talk. We tried for six months, and by the January of the year you would graduate, we had completed all the infertility workups. They told us "you are fine, go home and practice." We were the right age to start a family. The move to Switzerland for your job comes ever closer that spring before you graduated. You went to Switzerland alone in June after you had finished your boards and had the big graduation with your family. You told me "I do not care if you come, I am going." And you left. Even though you had seen the tumor on my breast from across the room, you left.

When I tell this story, I focus on him coming back from Switzerland after the cancer diagnosis. If I reflect on his words after he saw the tumor, the pain returns in full force. What kind of person says that? What kind of husband would leave his wife to deal with the full brunt of a potential cancer diagnosis on her own? Marriages come apart during crisis: the death of a child, infidelity, loss of income, or severe illness in one spouse. I know this to be true, but if you are the person who does not leave during crisis, this is devastating. I remember him striding across the room—the window open to welcome a cool breeze—coming close to see it because I had never shown him the lump. I remember lying in the bed after he had felt it and looked at the location of the visible tumor on my right breast. His heart's ugliness was revealed to me when he said, "I am going." I did not even cry or argue. I was totally still in my fully revealed aloneness.

Let no one deceive you with empty words, for because of these things the wrath of God comes upon the sons of disobedience. (Ephesians 5:6, NASB)

CHAPTER 6
DECEPTIVE: REGRETS FROM THE PAST

Infertility came before cancer. Before he graduated that spring, Tom found an opportunity to combine all of his degrees into one job. The job was in Switzerland. I had never imagined myself living overseas but was certainly intrigued. We spent time with the Swiss who were at the university, and since they spoke English and were even intermarried with Americans, I was at least willing to consider it.

Bible study was a big part of my spiritual growth during those four years of his dental school. I told a lady that I was possibly moving to Switzerland, and before I knew it, she had me interviewing to be a leader and start a class there. There were changes in lifestyle we had to make, and my husband was supportive. Alcohol and cigarettes had been a part of our entire married life, but that would stop. He knew that if we moved to Switzerland, and I gave up my career, it would be good for me if I could accomplish something in my time there. Starting a Bible study class would keep me busy.

We completed the infertility tests with a hysterosalpingogram. For this challenging test, they blow air into the fallopian tubes to see if there is blockage. Side effects are minimal, except for the shoulder pain that comes from the air bubbles migrating upward when you stand after the procedure. There were no issues regarding either him or me.

Lying on the bed one evening in the spring, I felt a lump on the outside of my right nipple. It was hard, but since I was trying to get pregnant, I let it go until the next month. At the time, I was meeting regularly with oncologists and radiation oncologists and surgeons regarding the design for a cancer treatment center. I was crazy busy with my hospital career. When my husband had completed his course work, graduated, and taken his boards, I thought it was time to tell him about the lump. We had not been very intimate during this crazy time in our lives.

He saw the lump that I found from across the bedroom. It was that big. He came and sat down on the bed beside me, asked if he could touch it. "You need to get into a doctor to see about a mammogram. You are only thirty, so it is unlikely that it is anything, but you need to get it checked while we have insurance." My job came in very handy in the next few months.

Tom left for Switzerland before the scheduled mammogram. Cancer was suspected and confirmed. The ultrasound, biopsy, and subsequent mastectomy occurred within a couple of days of the "bad" mammogram, when I was alone with friends and family. I went through that experience with another "God with skin on" friend named Pam. Tom and I had rented our house to other students, and I was living with another friend until I moved to Switzerland. I had sold both vehicles but had to renege on one of the sales. All of our things were in storage. My husband had just moved into an apartment in Switzerland and started a new job. I had just resigned my position and I had cancer. I was thirty years old. Alone.

I did not know if my husband would even return, His words before he left stayed in my mind.

I had worked to put him through dental school, buy his supplies, own a house, and pay for all our expenses. When he said he did not care whether I came with him to Switzerland, I remembered the last four years and wondered, "Have I been used? Taken? And will I now be discarded?" I still had the white turntable from my college years in our little house. It sat on a silver metal stand in the living room. When I came home from work, I would play the Wham! band album over and over and dance.

"Everything She Wants" by Wham! was my theme song for those last two years of Tom's schooling before he moved to Switzerland. It gives the flavor of financially, emotionally, and physically supporting someone who always wanted more.

> Somebody tell me
> Why I work so hard for you.

Journal

August 30, 1992

Second letter written to husband during separation.

My emotions have swung from disgust and relief to aching for your presence this last week. I hate you for your anger and your seeming craziness. I have yet to be able to forgive you. I have taken a mental trip into my imagination in order to discover what I need that I have not received from you. I brought Jesus with me to identify and give me those needs.

I need caring, gentle words, and a kind touch on my face, and to hear the words "I love you." The times that have surfaced in my memories of hurting the most are when you called me a f...bitch. Verbal abuse is the wound that Jesus must heal. God loves you and forgives you as a child of God who accepted Christ as his Savior, but I will not forgive you yet.

I make plenty of mistakes. I am bossy, but I respond childlike to kind rebuke. I do not respond well to your criticism like I was a child. This is not a parent-child relationship that someone must control in order to "win." Marriage should be our haven from the world mentality of competitiveness. You married a strong woman who has many feminine needs that have gone unmet in this marriage. I need kissing, affection, loving hugs, and affirmation of my unique femaleness. You made me self-conscious about my body (any extra weight must be exercised away, and I cannot have curves.) There is no kissing on the mouth—it was dirty (neurotic dentist issue.)

You accused me of being raised like a boy, having a man's job in a man's world. Add that to breast cancer and infertility and you could not wound my feminine side any deeper. But God created me in the womb, and I am fearfully and wonderfully made. He made me a woman with sexual needs, desires, and to be strong mentally and physically. He made me attractive to other humans, both my inside being and my outside appearance. You do not or cannot appreciate my womanhood, but that is your problem, not mine.

I now have a better understanding of your bisexuality/homosexuality tendencies. You have not acted upon these desires, to my knowledge, for years, but the repression of that truth about yourself is causing many physical and psychological problems for you. I cannot even deal with this within our marriage, because I believe I have known for a long time that something was not right, but just considered it your weird hang-ups. Of course you would want me to be bony thin; to have meat on those bones makes me have feminine curves.

I thought it was me. You needed me to think that, so you would have someone to blame for your unhappiness. I feel sorry for you, but you must resolve these issues of identity yourself. I am out of the way, but why did you marry me and keep me in the marriage relationship for so long? More importantly, why did I not know all this was not normal and I needed to get out?

There has been very little personal adjustment for me, as you had not been sleeping in bed with me, not having sex with me, and working evenings. The only difference I can feel in my aloneness is I have less stress. I am not constantly obsessed with providing the right food at the right time. I no longer worry about how the house looks, when you are coming home, and now you are in control of your own environment completely.

I miss our friendship, our companionship, our talks, similar interests, and fun things we liked to do together. I do not miss your obsessions, perfectionism, and critical spirit or self-focus. I became selfish too—in order to survive. Will we have restoration of our marriage? I do not know. We must first repair ourselves before we can consider blending our lives again. I may decide that I cannot "go back," cannot trust you again. There must be complete changes in your behavior and how you treat me, tested in anger-provoking circumstances over time and with the stress of family involvement before I would reconcile.

If you decide to divorce, I will be sad, because it is a death of my dreams of growing old with you. I will not file for divorce, even with the circumstances. I dreamed of walking, traveling, entertaining, watching movies with you. If you desire children of your own, then you must face a divorce first. I may not or probably cannot give children to you, and you have delayed action on adoption so long that now I must face childlessness alone also.

Fix yourself, resolve your issues including your parental issues, exorcise your demons, and I will be doing the same things. Do nothing, and I will grow right past you.

Depression is anger turned inward. Even though I understood that I couldn't make him be someone else or even to love me the way I should be loved, I felt angry that I had failed. The sadness of this realization was turned inward and I went to the doctor to get medication for the anxiety and depression. My brain did not function well and my thoughts were not rational at times. When I lived with Tom with all these issues, I began to be mentally ill. When all was revealed, I had no mental resources left to deal with the deception. I had anger, but I turned it inward on myself. I was clinically depressed.

Charm is deceitful and beauty is vain, but a woman who fears the Lord, she shall be praised. (Proverbs 31:30, NASB)

CHAPTER 7
PRETENSE: REMEMBRANCES

Tom did return from Switzerland to be with me after my cancer diagnosis. He had only been gone a couple of weeks, started his new job, and moved into the apartment. I was not sure he would return, considering what he said when he left town. During the next few months, I worked full time at my hastily rearranged job as I continued building a cancer center for a hospital. I took chemotherapy every month and recovered from surgeries and reconstruction implants. He went to work at the university, and friends helped us reestablish our disrupted lives. It was hard. We were scared. I was sick. He was trying. He bought me jewelry.

Seven months after my cancer diagnosis, we were on a plane to Switzerland, this time together. We packed to leave only five days after my final reconstruction surgery. I was exhausted from six months of Cytoxan, methotrexate, and 5FU (fluorouracil) chemotherapy. It is funny how you never forget the name of those incredible drugs. My doctors were concerned that I was leaving so soon after surgery and treatment, but the only thing my plastic surgeon told me was "Don't ski any this season."

We landed in Zurich with our overstuffed army duffle bags. The sight of the armed guards with Uzis was disconcerting. Because my husband spoke fluent German, we went through customs quickly. We sent the bags on to Bern and boarded the train. I was basically non-functional from exhaustion, stress, and jet lag, so he took very good care of our things and of me. We moved into the tiny, tiny apartment that he had stayed in for those two weeks, and I slept for days.

Excitement over shared experiences and survival kept us going for several weeks, and then I crashed. Clinical depression set in, and for six weeks, I could not function other than to do some grocery shopping. Tom had to do everything. I just lay in bed, cried, slept, and repeated it all over again. My friend's breast cancer had metastasized, and I did go to meet her at Medjugorje, Yugoslavia, the place where people have seen visions of the Mother Mary. That journey is all I remember from that time period. I was not fun to be around, people treated me like a fragile ill person, and Tom loved his life in Switzerland. I was mentally broken and sad.

My journal entries have helped me remember how I tried to keep our marriage together. We lived in Switzerland for three years after my cancer diagnosis and Tom's graduation. I immersed myself in Bible study and Christian reading to try to keep my marriage from spiraling into divorce. Tom took trips to England and Ireland, and at the time, I thought nothing of it. At one point, I was tempted to have an affair in Rome. Our remarkable experiences in our travels to different countries kept us from focusing on our relationship. Ups and downs of marriage in a foreign country are common. With one of us starting a ministry, we were both faced with the spiritual attacks. The enemy was unacknowledged, and the Evil One worked on two very challenged, physically and emotionally ill individuals. My journal entries are a raw, distant, and searing testimony to a Christian woman doing anything she can to save her marriage. I wrote these words three years before my separation, before I realized Tom was gay. I would give the same readings to anyone going through a difficult time in their marriage.

It was a final, desperate, and futile attempt to keep my sanity after the experience of cancer, dental school and relocation to a foreign country. After we arrived in Switzerland, I made no journal entries for more than a year.

Journal

April 1, 1989

I woke up happy with good dreams and pleasant thoughts. A rare treat. My prayer time was to speak to God 90 minutes per day, allowing me to pray for more people. My husband's mother called and cussed at him last night. She believes he is being influenced, as he is different. She was irrational, so he hung up on her. How can they repair this relationship? He defended his father's inability to stand up to her, and so my husband is now attacking his daddy.

Because our English television is very limited, I watched the Invisible Man or Shadow Man on *Twilight Zone*, and it really affected my sleep and dreams. The little girl is at Grandpa's house looking out the window when she sees Shadow Man and feels the evil presence. I want to verify the evil and see black smoke. Then Jesus comes and is floating between this house and our car. I woke up and thought of Philippians 4:7, "And the peace of God which passes all understanding shall guard your heart and mind in Christ Jesus." I prayed with thanksgiving.

My husband talked to his father finally and seems to have resolved the hurt feelings. He thinks his Mom is too crazy to act rationally, and he doesn't even want to talk to her. He is still mad at me because I wouldn't talk this time when we had guests who were speaking German, and he had to explain why I was too nervous to be left alone.

Journal

April 8, 1989

After being in bed for twelve hours and asleep for ten, I decided to move myself. I am in a bitchy mood, and my husband is tired after little sleep for days. He is constantly saying nasty comments. It is a good thing I am gone for this wedding most of the day. One day, I didn't pick up or wash dishes and the place is a wreck because it is so small. I had an erotic dream with my husband. I'm sure it has been over a week since I had any desire, so at least I am not dead. He and I are on some different wavelength now. I don't want him around very much, so I ignore him. I must look at myself to see why. Everything in life is such a bother to him unless he receives new stimuli or is entertained. So much of my life is quiet and boring, and I feel he should learn to entertain himself.

Journal

April 15, 1989

A nice slow relaxing weekend ahead for us, which is the last one for many weeks. Pam, our good friend who helped us when I was diagnosed with cancer, will be here from Anchorage, Alaska, in one week. Will she recognize this calmer, changed, deeply religious person I have become? How will I view her career obsession? Our mutual friend, Jana, is pregnant again, how fortunate for her. Will it ever be me? Will God give me the desires of my heart, or is there never to be children? I must "delight" myself in the Lord, as I was shown again today. Only as I see how much I enjoy studying God's word do I see the beauty of my ability to teach and know more. Oh, God, let me see through the crack in the door.

Journal

May 11, 1989

So much has happened in the last month, but first let me concentrate on today. I am sitting on a sand dune, listening to the ocean off the coast of Sweden. Halmstad—a small town where my husband is finishing his lecture. Nature, so beautiful and serene, makes me sing songs of worship and praise. To sit in the pews of St. Nickolai and pray quietly, certainly gives the feeling of unity with all Christians. Why is it still so hard for me to rest in the Lord and relax? I feel bored because I have walked around and slowly studied the people. It's hard not to understand anyone again, but the people are warm and friendly. They have a special society of socialism here.

Flashback to Italy—Pam's Visit

I remember him. The first man I almost had an affair with after eight years of an unsatisfactory marriage and a cancer diagnosis. He was gorgeous, flirtatious and attentive in every way, and my interest was an indication that things were not good at home. It started when my friend visited my husband and me in Switzerland just a little less than two years from when she was with me for my first cancer diagnosis in Texas.

Pam was a successful executive living in Anchorage, Alaska, and we had worked together for a few years before we bonded over our shared Christian Church heritage and my cancer experience. She was funny, could cope on her own, found the apartment in Bern, even after jet lag from flying across the Arctic Circle, and she was thrilled to be in Europe for her first time.

Did I even know what I needed when I boarded the train to Rome? After 10 hours, we arrived on a holiday, so few rooms were available. Our 'pension' or small room was close to the Melrose station, and we stayed there for four nights. After finding the right train station, the boys found us! Singing, gorgeous, Italian boys. Pam has beautiful red hair, and my blond hair had its own attractions, but the two of us stood out in a crowd of mostly dark-haired beauties. Pam was still coping with the language issue and would just go up to someone and ask, "Hi, can I have a bus plan?" We boarded a bus and off to the Campidoglio. From the first view of the Roman Coliseum, I was hooked again on Italy. It was my third time to visit in fifteen months of living in Switzerland.

Up to the Roman Forum at dusk, just like Frommer's Travel Guide said to do, with just a small fear of the unknown. Looking for the statue of Marcus Aurelius with the pedestal by Michelangelo, we were asked by two guys if they could borrow our map. They said, "Are you Americans?" and I came out of a fog two days later. Pam was not married, and was very protective of her friend's marriage and, especially, of my fragility. The guys gave us a personal tour of the Forum, Appian Way, and standing on the coin for a wish for a "long and healthy life" started out our evening. We visited Paul's prison, Julius Caesar's house, and the Palatine Hill, all described to us by the two Romans who really did not need a map for their own city. We drank coffee and espresso and had Pam's first of many gelatos. She braves the experience with me and takes a tour of Rome, including going to a nightclub for some dancing with the Romans. All the young kids we saw were drinking and smoking at no more than thirteen years old. Pam tried Campari and we teased Gianfranco about all the smoking. I remember a sensual tan suede coat.

The plans are all set, and we go to bed at 2:00 a.m. after getting up at 5:00 a.m. the day before, knowing that this has already been a special trip. We saw the Vatican during a Papal audience and are overwhelmed with the numbers of Italians in uniforms, all trying to be so "helpful" to the Americans. The art, Raphael rooms, and the Sistine Chapel required a reverence and a new understanding of what is important in Italian history and art. We visited St. Peter's Basilica to stare at the Pieta, now protected from crazy people with protective Plexiglas after someone had broken off part of the statue years before. I said my prayers for the friend with brain metastasis from breast cancer, and kept my vow to keep speaking with God, even on vacation.

We went back to the Hotel Pension to rest and prepare for another night out with Paul and Gianfranco. This time, they took us to one of the Seven Hills to look over the city and the Tiber River. The smell of orange blossoms was heavenly as was the touch of Gianfranco's hand on my elbow guiding me to the views. We walked up to a keyhole that requires you to lean over to see through it. But when you do, it is a view in the distance directly of St. Peter's Basilica, all hazy on a cloudy night. Most tourists never see these secret places, and I could not find them again. When we travel, we all have moments that stand out in our memories, and I call these "moments to remember."

We took walks to a quiet place of Rome that added to the wonder of the city. We continued to supper with a Margarhita pizza, first with an appetizer of fried rice with tomatoes. These guys were nice, spoke English well, and were, so far, not expecting anything more than our company. Near the Pantheon, Gianfranco gives a sucker to a gypsy child, and we get espresso from a nearby coffee bar. Pam almost pukes on the strong Espresso and laughs about how she just thought she "hated American coffee" until she tried Espresso. I think that Gianfranco cannot read English, because he says he doesn't understand all the "no smoking" signs. They were there just for the tourists. The Pantheon, with its 2,000 years of history with all the traditional Roman round arches around the square, was overwhelming to me in the wash of my emotions. I just leaned my cheek against the cool stone and had another "moment to remember."

A Brazilian singer with a Latin beat was a divine finish to the evening. We had some danc-ing together, met a Peruvian fellow and talked about life, love, and moments that take your breath away. Why I responded to such warm and living attention is something that required much thought. I just knew I was alive, a woman, desired, and it was superb. Pam told me much later that she had prayed "protection" around me for those two nights and two days, and I was left with only a kiss. But it was a good one, and God knows, I was glad and sad the Italian man was in Rome and I was in Switzerland.

Journal

May 31, 1989

Yesterday was our eighth anniversary. My husband came home for lunch and brought eight roses with white flowers and baby's breath, a perfect anniversary bouquet. What dreams and hopes there were at the beginning and what we expected our life to be has changed to include the uncertainty of my life and our future together. Yes, he still loves me very much. We stayed home with candlelight and Swiss *forelle blau* trout cooked to perfection. Then the best lovemaking we had had in a long while. Maybe we will never celebrate "out" again? Where will we be next year? Truly, God only knows.

I was finally able to say to him, I am willing to go back to America and pay for our house by working, or I was willing to stay in Switzerland. We had to rent our house out in one month, or I had to make plans to return to San Antonio and take care of things. It was just too much to leave to others. Oh, when will I get pregnant? Everyone seems to be expecting or having healthy babies.

Reading the Psalms gives me such joy. They make you rely on the all-powerful God, maker of the incredible Alps. We saw the Matterhorn both days we were in Zermatt with our other visitors, which is unusual. We traveled across the Simplon Pass and the most incredible scenery of the Alps and the road through them. After overnighting (not a good English word for the German *ubernacht*) in Stresa, Italia, we traveled to Cannobio to shop. Then back through Locarno, Switzerland, to Bellinzona, Switzerland, for lunch. The tunnel was closed, so we had to go over the Gotthard Pass—a fabulous road with so many hairpin curves you could not sit up straight before you curved into the next one. We stopped in Luzern for only an hour before returning to Bern. We traveled 600 kilometers in two-and-a-half days, but my body was still traveling in the borrowed Mercedes all night.

Journal

Sunday, June 4, 1989

What is happening in the world? Khomeini dies? Poland's free elections? Russia's openness? Lord, what are you preparing now?

Prayers of women in the Bible for children: Genesis 18:14 Sarah. "Is anything too difficult for the Lord" Genesis 21:6. "And Sarah said, 'God has made laughter for me; everyone who hears will laugh with me.'" 1 Samuel 1:11 Hannah says, "O Lord of Hosts, if Thou wilt indeed look on the affliction of Thy maidservant and remember me, and not forget Thy maidservant, but will give Thy maidservant a son, then I will give him to the Lord all the days of his life." "She gave birth to three more sons and two daughters."

Journal

June 12, 1989

The Alpine view of a Sunday afternoon includes hikers with their dog on the path in front of the Swiss Chalet, white walled and brown roofed, slanted for the winter snow. Tinkle. Tinkle. Tinkle. The cows with their beautiful silver bells compete for attention, as the cows are as clean and beautiful as the surroundings. There are silver-tipped mountains in the background that drip down to trees and verdant valleys. The orchestra of cowbells, the purple and yellow of wildflowers in an alpine meadow match with the majesty of mountains feeding water into pristine, clear streams. We hiked up one-and-one-half hours from Champery. After hours with this view as a backdrop, we crossed a mountain and stopped at the summit. We truly needed hiking boots as we hiked over the summit to see Champery in the distance. Through meadows, forests, cow pastures with shepherdesses along the sides of steep hills back to Champery. Only our memories will last past this moment. Thank you for our bodies and our senses and our memories. What is St. Peter saying to us about the "devil is a roaring lion"? I see him more often as quietly standing like a lamb, deceiving us in our minds.

Journal

June 15, 1989

My husband and I have fought for two weeks. No sex, no communication, only anger since he returned from Champery. I told him this morning, "I'm feeling neglected." He either has his nose in a German book or glued to TV or asleep in the evening. I have been discontent, and then my husband just wants to stay away from me.

I tell him I am interested in sex, stand before him naked, and nothing. He doesn't want sex; I don't think it is I. What can I do to liven up our relationship? Soon I will be reading all those self-help magazines! I believe we love each other, but it is just slow. We must speak to one another, touch, relate, and our closeness comes through circles to intimacy and back to sex.

Complaining does nothing, so I must try more constructive methods of attack. I hope I get some inspiration.

Journal

June 30, 1989

My husband has been in Ireland since Tuesday, and I have not even been lonely yet. I have spent time with lovely women I have met here. The time has gone quickly, and what a precious time it has been. I believe I have experienced healing emotionally and to test my faith and healing by working again. I'm no longer "biding my time," because that is "wasting my time," and it is too precious to waste. Oh, God, I want your blessing and your peace. I want the healing that is possible only through forgiving others and myself. I praise you Lord for what you have done for me in the last 30 days, even if it is painful.

Journal

July 7, 1989

Two-year Anniversary of Cancer Diagnosis

My husband thinks we should tour England before we leave Europe. He enjoyed his time in Ireland very much, but there is much more to see. There is so much more to understand about his Ireland experience. Even though we had company that night, it didn't stop a really wonderful "homecoming." Will this week apart really have improved our perspective? Will getting a job help me? Money pressures are gone, praise to God. Abundance, as always, when we give, we receive. "Oh, Lord, let me be generous with my money for you Lord" is my prayer.

Journal

August 10, 1989

Is God speaking to me through dreams? Maybe not, but I must have pleasant nights. A few nights ago, I awoke with the dream of a small boy two years or so sitting on my lap. He was mine! But not mine. Perhaps adopted. I felt so peaceful and loved. I am scared of the pregnancy risks, especially with no cancer-specific insurance. Maybe I wasn't so ready. Perhaps this was sent to comfort and encourage me to consider adoption.

Journal

August 13, 1989

Tom told me last night, "I love you, Debi." It had been such a long time, and I will treasure it.

Journal

August 20, 1989

One more week until work begins for me. I am scared and thrilled, and three months will be tough as I learn the job and the language. I had one bad dream last week, which took place after a circus. A man, evil-looking, turns and looks at me with such hate in his eyes. Last night, I prayed and praised God before bed, and God gave me Galatians 5:18. "If we live by the Spirit, we also must walk in the Spirit." I have resentment over our separate bedrooms. I don't want him to touch me; I don't feel close to him. We had an angry day and evening, so I prayed for him and myself and our marriage. This morning had a special quietness.

His back and stomach are both really bothering him. He had returned from Ireland two months prior and been bothered with stomach problems since. I believe he is going to another doctor this week. I wonder if he prays for himself. Probably not. The demon of tiredness kept me in bed and not to church. My husband said he would go with me, because I go with him to things.

Tom's trip to Ireland was the beginning of the end. When I visited beautiful Ireland many years later, I remembered his love for this area. It is an easy country to love. The people are so funny and friendly, the green is vibrant, and history and culture are everywhere. He had all these strange stomach symptoms after his return from Ireland. I was settling into Switzerland, had a new job, friends, Bible study, hiking, and a renewed calm in the marriage. The adjustment period was over and we loved living in Switzerland. There was one thing lacking—honesty.

The heart is more deceitful than all else and is desperately sick; Who can understand it? (Jeremiah 17:9, NASB)

CHAPTER 8
DISINFORMATION: RESOLVE

I rented a cabin in the mountains to retreat while my husband went to a dental conference in Cardiff, Wales, in England for the second time in just a few months. I heard about this place from friends and decided that God and I were going to do battle during this weekend. Divorce loomed after nine months of relative quiet. Infertility was all I thought about, and my desire for a child overpowered his verbal and emotional cruelty. I wrote pages and pages of notes from the Bible, Christian teachers, and tapes I listened to while there.

A lady who had spent time there learning more about God bought the cabin near L'Abri ministry. She then served the ministry until her death, when she left the cabin and all her possessions to the ministry. She had books on every challenging topic of life and even left her personal Bible with her notes on her studies in it. There was a small kitchen, and it was just a short walk up the valley to visit L'Abri.

L'Abri is located in the small Alpine village of Huémoz, Canton de Vaud, and overlooks the Rhone valley, surrounded by the magnificent Alps. From Geneva it is a one-and-one-half-hour train journey to the town of Aigle, followed by a winding trip by bus up the mountainside to L'Abri.

The French term L'Abri translates in English as "the shelter." It is an international study center and a residential community. In 1955, Francis and Edith Schaeffer, the founders of the work, opened their chalet/home to those who sought answers to life's many questions, and L'Abri began.

L'Abri continues to provide a place where people can be part of an extended family, receive honest answers to honest questions, and cultivate or pursue the truth of Christianity.

Journal

May 4, 1990

Huemoz, Switzerland, at L'Abri

Green, lush grass and pasture. An apple blossom, white dandelion, with a backdrop of brown and white cows is truly a pastoral scene. I'm packed up with food and clothes for three days alone. God will help me conquer the fear. Lord, this weekend is for the two of us. Solitude and forced no contact with people. Reading, listening to Your voice. My husband is deciding whether he wants to stay married or be alone. He knows he doesn't want children. I have also fought the demon of divorce this week. I wondered where the next spiritual attack would come from, and now I know. I have rebuked this in my mind, because God gave me the scripture, "Wife must not separate from her husband." Painful, but true. He said some really hurtful things, but I just keep forgiving the criticism and anger, knowing that only God can change him, not me. He kissed me good-bye as he left for Cardiff. I plan to chronicle this spiritual weekend—stronger and ready to face what You want me to see and do.

Notes from L'Abri

Marriage:
> Designed to alleviate loneliness
> Planned to bring happiness, not misery
> Must begin by leaving all relationships:
> Leave, Cleave, Become One Flesh

Whatever is important to you should be less important than your marriage. Test every action, attitude, and word. Will this build up our relationship or tear it down? Will this draw us closer or drive us apart? Does it reveal my love and loyalty to my partner, or does it reveal my self-centered individualism?

1. Man and woman chose each other, but God joins them. Do not keep divorce in your vocabulary or your mind. It hinders and sabotages any attempts to improve the relationship.
2. Separateness is from Satan—God joins things, and togetherness is Biblical.
3. Love is defined in God's word as everlasting and wanting to do the best for the one we love. Ephesians 5 and 1 Corinthians 13
4. Love can be learned—it is not simple, it is an art. Learn principles and practice them daily.
5. Love is a power that will produce love as I give it, not try to attract it.
6. Love is a choice—just as Happiness. Deliberately choosing to give myself to my husband, trusting that good feelings come after changing behaviors.

"Even the bird does not rest on her branch alone, but seeks others to sing with."

Courage—seeking the time and energy to try to continue this marriage.

What are the consequences of a separation to me and to Bible study? In the early 1990s, Bible study, under executive leadership, sought to increase its international presence, especially in capitals of different countries. The hope was to reach a greater number of English speakers in the diplomatic circles and to minister to all the English-speaking employees of the different embassies. I had been trained to start a class in Bern, Switzerland, when I lived in Texas and had been through almost three years of teas, coffees, interim Bible studies, support from England's leadership, and other Swiss classes in order to have enough people to sustain a class in Bern.

The consequences to me, personally, of a separation and divorce were that I could not be a "teaching leader" per Bible study guidelines. Because of the counseling involved in this discipleship ministry, the stance of this particular Bible study group was to discourage divorce. Their desire not to cause undue stress to a divorcing leader meant I would have to resign if we separated. The guidelines were clear, and this was one of the reasons I was determined to make the marriage work. I believed in the ministry. I knew the battle for the hearts and minds of these women would be set back if the leader divorced. The prayer support of the team in Bern would be absent from my life, and I did not know how I would survive without it.

Journal from time at L'Abri

Lawrence Crabb—"Biblical Counseling/Basic Principles"—Notes from my Journal

Identify negative feelings produced by wrongful thinking.

Wrongful thinking—always involves the sinful belief that something more than God and His provisions is necessary for meeting one's needs.

God is totally sufficient for me! But we say, "I need to have my way in order to be happy."

Belief: I can be fulfilled only if my wife (or husband) exhibits devotion, thus giving wife (or husband) the power to make him happy or unhappy.

Belief: I have a right to be happy. Neglectful behavior is seen as his right and may be violated. Basic needs:

1. Man is made in God's image—God of the Bible is both personal and infinite.

2. Most psychological symptoms (anxiety, depression, uncontrolled temper, lying, sexual problems) are either direct result or defensive attempts to cope with unmet personal needs.

3. Marriage applications: Wife—has loving needs not being met. Husband—wrong belief— "I am a man only if I never give in to another's demands." Anxiety is fear of domination.

4. Resentment—against the wife for trying to control. Wife—turns up the pressure and becomes frustrated manipulator. Husband—resists demands by angrily withdrawing and may become adulterer. Wife—change her approach to make no demands. Husband is free to be nicer. The wrong beliefs continue whenever either wife or husband does not get their own way.

5. Be responsible for what each can control and need to die to the sin pattern in my own life. Decide to believe and persevere to put off sin and put on righteousness.

6. Before embarking on behavior change, each must decide "no" to sin. Confess and repent the sin as they are revealed to you, and then reject that sin. Our goal must be to become more Christ-like.

I was trying to change myself and find a reason to stay. At the time, I was still under the illusion that I could change myself and make everything all right. When I re-read these notes: "Wife—change her approach to make no demands." Seriously? Did I believe that he would be nicer to me if I did that?

Notes from my Journal

"Love Must be Tough"—James Dobson

Look for subtle changes
One partner feels trapped
Becomes non-communicative
Provokes continuous fights over insignificant issues
Refuses counseling or help
Primary ingredient of midlife crisis

"He tries to escape, and I am announcing Biblically I will not leave him."

1. The best chance is to pull backwards slightly.
2. Demands are made for loyalty, service, commitment, and they want escape and freedom.
3. Grownups still love the chase, the unattainable.
4. Commitment given insufficient attention. It dies if there is too much attachment as well.
5. Respect—the value one ascribes to the other and the vulnerable partner opens the "cage" door.

6. Loving discipline that requires them to make a choice between alternatives. There must be mutual accountability.
7. Pray first, go where the Holy Spirit leads, and go into the "harbor of God's infinite love."
8. The partner must be tough but loving—the demanding partner cannot have it both ways.
9. Request the prayer of every believer who knows and love the family under fire.
10. The "smothered" partner will find instant relief if you express your limits and show self-respect and confidence. If you love him unconditionally, he will push to be proved unlovable.
11. Do not take moving out lightly.
12. Don't talk too much. Don't share your tears.
13. Change your behavior—be quiet; don't always tell him every little incident of your day. He doesn't tell you everything.
14. Only telephone him with business. DO NOT resort to verbal brawls. If he insults you—make your response crisp, controlled, and confident. Tell him nothing.
15. Do NOT behave unlovingly—build bridges.
16. He is losing his best friend—not just his wife.
17. Have a counselor to walk you through it.

If they return:

1. Written commitment to counseling long term.
2. Major spiritual commitment in the family.
3. Try unbelievably hard to make them happy.

God gave us a conscience, which nags at us with guilt over sin. Internal conflict between conscience and actual behavior can cause physical illness.

Unconditional love is not synonymous with passivity, permissiveness, or weakness.

Rejection by the one you love is the most powerful destroyer of self-esteem in all-human experience. Get ready to do battle with Satan.

Line of respect—when he shouts disrespect to me at anytime, I will not sit passively, but will clearly tell him he has crossed my line. (He had done this twice regarding a table setting and a dirty house.)

Knowing my spiritual obligations, he feels entitled to do as he pleases. Focus on the exact behavior that is not appropriate.

I needed a counselor in order to maintain the marriage and my sanity. "He tries to escape, and I announce Biblically, I will not leave him." I did that. He knew how important God and the Bible study were to me, so he could do as he pleased. I was miserable. He was more miserable. I see now that he had massive secrets, pain, and shame. My hope was that our love could survive and our friendship would sustain this tough time. How could I not see that he could not change? He could not.

"Love Must Be Tough" Chapter 14, *Angry Women, Passive Men*—James Dobson

1. He feels his responsibility ends with providing and being loyal like Dad.
2. She expects romance and emotional attachment.
3. He hides, becomes silent, and watches TV. She becomes angrier and feels powerless and disrespected.
4. She refuses to attend office business functions or show support for his profession. Tells

stories to church associates, and shuts him down sexually.

5. He doesn't meet her sexual needs and is a workaholic.
6. She can't expect him to make her happy or vice versa. Extreme independence can also be destructive.
7. Pull backward—appear to need him less. Show appreciation for what he does right. But first you must notice it. Be happy and fun to be with.
8. Sex is best when it runs hot and cold.
9. Don't verbalize your every thought. If you communicate too much and there is no mystery, only bare day-to-day ugliness.

We discredit that with which we are stuck, and we lust for what is beyond our grasp.

I took these notes because they described my marriage. It seemed counterintuitive to back away, give him space, and allow him to return as he could. I did this for several months, and things did get better. The fights were less intense, but the physical love was non-existent.

Journal

May 5, 1990

Huemoz, Switzerland L'Abri

Spiritual answers received today: Until I am Lord of your LIFE, you will not receive the desires of your heart. Health, future, children, give them up? And now give up my marriage, Bible study leadership? Give it and the effects to God.

Will God make heaven more beautiful than Switzerland in the spring? Seeing mountains, snow topped, red, yellow, and blue forget-me-nots, lambs and baby cows with their mommas. Oh, what gifts you give me, even if it takes something like this to make me dependent on you.

After listening to Marriage Tapes at L'Abri by Edith Schaeffer, I made comments after each scripture. I am more convicted that there is so much more I need to do to repair my marriage, and God is not "letting" me out for now.

Mrs. Schaeffer: The source of all our actions and beliefs is that we are somebody and our lives matter to God.

"Go to the ant, you sluggard; consider its ways and be wise! It has no commander, no overseer or ruler, yet it stores its provisions in summer and gathers its food at harvest. How long will you lay there, you sluggard? When will you get up from your sleep? A little sleep, a little slumber, a little folding of the hands to rest" (Proverbs 9: 6–10, NIV).

Mrs. Schaeffer: Leave your simple ways and live focused on the Word of God. Focus not on twisted ideas but on what God has said. Wait to hear from him because we intend to act. Listening to God's word and understand we sit "under" the Word not level with it.

Lose your life to find it and put yourself aside, day to day in marriage.

"The LORD God said, "It is not good for the man to be alone. I will make a helper suitable for him." Now the LORD God had formed out of the ground all the beasts of the field and all the birds of the air. He brought them to the man to see what he would name them; and whatever the man called each living creature, that was its name. So the man gave names to all the livestock, the birds of the air and all the beasts of the field. But for Adam no suitable helper was found. So the LORD God caused the man to fall into a deep sleep; and while he was sleeping, he took one of the man's ribs and closed up the place with flesh. Then the LORD God made a woman from the rib he had taken out of the man, and he brought her to the man. The man said, "This is now bone of my bones and flesh of my flesh; she shall be called "woman," for she was taken out of man." For this reason a man will leave his father and mother and be united to his wife, and they will become one flesh. The man and his wife were both naked, and they felt no shame" (Genesis 2:18–25, NIV).

Mrs. Schaeffer: God is personal, and therefore, the created being-man desires personal contact. Adam states this longing as a reality. The creator of the universe could have decided not to form woman. Instead He formed her as part of man but diverse. There was perfectness, physical oneness, and total equality. Their bond was immediate, spiritual oneness with no one being higher or lower than the other—they were blended.

"Wives, submit to your husbands as to the Lord. For the husband is the head of the wife as Christ is the head of the church, his body, of which he is the Savior. Now as the church submits to Christ, so also wives should submit to their husbands in everything. Husbands, love your wives, just as Christ loved the church and gave himself up for her to make her holy, cleansing her by the washing with water through the word, and to present her to himself as a radiant church, without stain or wrinkle or any other blemish, but holy and blameless. In this same way, husbands ought to love their wives as their own bodies. He who loves his wife loves himself. After all, no one ever hated his own body, but he feeds and cares for it, just as Christ does the church—for we are members of his body. For this reason a man will leave his father and mother and be united to his wife, and the two will become one flesh. This is a profound mystery—but I am talking about Christ and the church. However, each one of you also must love his wife as he loves himself, and the wife must respect her husband" (Ephesians 5:22–32, NIV).

Mrs. Schaeffer. Women are trying to be like men when their drives are different. We as Christian women are to teach men as only the bride of Christ. The preciousness of these differences should be cherished—feminine and masculine. You are not married to the same person through the years because they change. How can you influence others if you cannot influence the one person you live with?

Pray for the changes continually, for creativity and good ideas if the person is willing. Be creative and have ideas about new things to do together that you enjoy—become kindred spirits. Intellectually—everything that is unspiritual; art, food, hobbies that cross over between two people in a marriage. Physically—attraction that leads to physical oneness.

There will not be a perfect marriage, because we are both imperfect people. Another person in a second or third marriage does not help the situation of this imperfect marriage. "I will live with this person with their faults and good points."

"If I speak in the tongues of men and of angels, but have not love, I am only a resounding gong or a clanging cymbal. If I have the gift of prophecy and can fathom all mysteries and all knowledge, and if I have a faith that can move mountains, but have not love, I am nothing. If I give all I possess to the poor and surrender my body to the flames, but have not love, I gain nothing. Love is patient, love is kind. It does not envy, it does not boast, it is not proud. It is not rude, it is not self-seeking, it is not easily angered, it keeps no record of wrongs. Love does not delight in evil but rejoices with the truth. It always protects, always trusts, always hopes, always perseveres. Love never fails" (1 Corinthians 13:1–8, NIV).

My thoughts: What is love? Am I showing too much faith in God and not enough love? Patience, long-suffering is how you can show love for the things that differ from your expectations. Kindness means saying "never mind," not saying the mean things, and having sensitivity.

Mrs. Schaeffer: Envy not—Equality is not the practice of love, it is not to be shared equally. We are not equal in strengths, talents or energy; we should not have a balance when it comes to showing love.

Not be puffed up—weakness in others gives us love opportunities. Before God I am a small creature. "I wouldn't do that," or, "I wouldn't say or act that way." Pray for the "speak up" to be removed and take our own failings away first before we notice others.

Not easily provoked—forgiveness of the person and practice saying, "I'm sorry." Rejoice not in iniquity, but rejoice in the truth—an awesome thought is to compliment the little things, and point out the things that are joyful and lovely.

Bears all things—this is not being a door-mat; this is the possibility of showing love if they tell the same story for the 79th time. Love never fails—lifetime is very short, but the time you are together never fails.

"Some Pharisees came to him to test him. They asked, "Is it lawful for a man to divorce his wife for any and every reason?" "Haven't you read," he replied, "that at the beginning the Creator 'made them male and female,' and said, 'For this reason a man will leave his father and mother and be united to his wife, and the two will become one flesh'? So they are no longer two, but one. Therefore what God has joined together, let man not separate." "Why then," they asked, "did Moses command that a man give his wife a certificate of divorce and send her away?" Jesus replied, "Moses permitted you to divorce your wives because your hearts were hard. But it was not this way from the beginning. I tell you that anyone who divorces his wife, except for marital unfaithfulness, and marries another woman commits adultery." The disciples said to him, "If this is the situation between a husband and wife, it is better not to marry." Jesus replied, "Not everyone can accept this word, but only those to whom it has been given" (Matthew 19:3–11, NIV).

Mrs. Schaeffer: If one person is unfaithful, he/she is permitted to remarry, as the person has walked away from the marriage covenant. Adultery is a broken relationship of the oneness of the marriage covenant. Marriage is to be a lasting relationship, but there is a possibility of more than one person in the circle of God, Husband, and Wife as in death or infidelity.

"Do you not know that your bodies are members of Christ himself? Shall I then take the members of Christ and unite them with a prostitute? Never! Do you not know that he who unites himself with a prostitute is one with her in body? For it is said, "The two will become one flesh." But he who unites himself with the Lord is one with him in spirit. Flee from sexual immorality. All other sins a man commits are outside his body, but he who sins sexually sins against his own body. Do you not know that your body is a temple of the Holy Spirit, who is in you, whom you have received from God? You are not your own; you were bought at a price. Therefore honor God with your body" (1 Corinthians 6:15–20, NIV).

Mrs. Schaeffer: Promiscuity is any form of sexual interaction before or outside of marriage. Our body is for the Lord, not for fornications. In the Resurrection—our bodies are not dead but raised also and will be with us in some form for eons of time. We as members of Christ body— would we unite with a prostitute? This would reflect the depth if they become one physically. The pure physical act makes people one—even without love or emotion. This is clearly stated as a sin and that even though these sins are covered with Christ's righteousness, we are to flee fornication. Our body is the temple of the Holy Spirit, and once you've accepted Christ as your Savior, you would grieve Him and the Holy Spirit and squash him by being in sexual sin.

"Now for the matters you wrote about: It is good for a man not to marry. But since there is so much immorality, each man should have his own wife, and each woman her own husband. The husband should fulfill his marital duty to his wife, and likewise the wife to her husband. The wife's body does not belong to her alone but also to her husband. In the same way, the husband's body does not belong to him alone but also to his wife. Do not deprive each other except by mutual consent and for a time, so that you may devote yourselves to prayer. Then come together again so that Satan will not tempt you because of your lack of self-control. I say this as a concession, not as a command. I wish that all men were as I am. But each man has his own gift from God; one has this gift, another has that. Now to the unmarried and the widows I say: It is good for them to stay unmarried, as I am. But if they cannot control themselves, they should marry, for it is better to marry than to burn with passion. To the married I give this command (not I, but the Lord): A wife must not separate from her husband. But if she does, she must remain unmarried or else be reconciled to her husband. And a husband must not divorce his wife. To the rest I say this (I, not the Lord): If any brother has a wife who is not a believer and she is willing to live with him, he must not divorce her. And if a woman has a husband who is not a believer and he is willing to live with her, she must not divorce him. For the unbelieving husband has been sanctified through his wife, and the unbelieving wife has been sanctified through her believing husband. Otherwise your children would be unclean, but as it is, they are holy. But if the unbeliever leaves, let him do so. A believing man or woman is not bound in such circumstances; God has called us to live in peace. How do you know, wife, whether you will save your husband? Or, how do you know, husband, whether you will save your wife?

Nevertheless, each one should retain the place in life that the Lord assigned to him and to which God has called him. This is the rule I lay down in all the churches" (1 Corinthians 7:1–17, NIV).

Mrs. Schaeffer: Paul is not asking people to live in asceticism, but refers back to 1 Corinthians Chapter 6, where they have already been promiscuous. Oneness is still necessary to avoid fornication. We live in a fallen world, and some of us aren't married. There is no perfection in the sexual relationship but there should be no submissiveness in sex for the wife. He speaks to the issue that sometimes the woman had greater sexual need and sometimes the man. Adultery was a theft of the body from the other person. Don't cheat each other, even in the imagination. Enhancement of time together, not saying you are sick, tired, depressed, and never acting in anger. It is an urgent thing in married life. If we are not fulfilling the needs of the other partner, then they are opened up to temptation. If they are too spiritual, foregoing any sexual interaction, they are also tempted. The wife is to be like the church—communicate with husband as the church communicates with the Lord. Make their needs known, and talk things over together. Togetherness needs time. Time for communication, shared work, influence each other, share books, be creative, listen to each other and grow in marriage. There is never a 50/50 in a marriage; sometimes it is 90/10 and sometimes 10/90, as long as it always adds up to 100% by both.

I was immersed in scriptures and teachings of wise Christian counsel. There were so many things I had done wrong. We had lived together for a few months before marriage. I was unskilled in things of passion and sexual intimacy. My desire to please him led him to run over me with ridiculous demands. Until I left after twelve years of marriage, I had never opened a can of beans to serve with our food. All the beans had to be dried, soaked, cooked, and then frozen, or he would not eat them. The joy of eating canned beans has never left me to this day.

I had a very sharp tongue, and even though I did everything I could to be "Christ-like," I was critical, manipulative, and rationalizing. I created the atmosphere of home but did not support Tom's choice of friends and career. I said that his friends were not "Christian" enough. Each of my critical comments hit like a sharp-edged hammer hooking into his head. I know now so much more about myself. I see how many of my issues had yet to be healed. But at that time, I was just trying to hold my marriage together, alone, and I did not understand what the issues were. I batted blindly into the darkest of nights. Rejection, divorce, childlessness, and cancer issues popped up and down like Jack-in-the-box dolls, and nothing would keep them contained. Terror consumed me.

Excerpt from L'Abri

A Growing Love, Ulrich Schaeffer

She was told to stick with him, to "bear" him, to be strong
        by his side.
She stayed with him through emotional abuse,
through his temper tantrums, through his irresponsibility.
She remained strong through it all.

Was her "bearing" him, as a good Christian wife should,
not her own twisted way of revenge,
because her 'holiness' was so hard for him to bear?
He lost faith in himself and saw himself as weak,
while she was strong,
and he resented her more and more,
but could not act on it
because she looked so right and he looked so wrong.

Perhaps an act of trust on her part would have been to let
   her temper flare,
show her weaknesses,
to refuse to be strong and be unable to bear everything.

Love matures,
As the lovability of the other
Disappears.

As I reread my journal years after the fact, my negative think-ing and my willingness to accept the entire fault, guilt, and shame for a non-working marriage saddens me. I found this poem in the writings at L'Abri, and nothing was more real to me than the words: "Perhaps an act of trust would be to show her weaknesses, to refuse to be strong, and be unable to bear everything." How boring to live with me, someone who is "holy" and always doing good for everyone while he fought all the demons alone. My hus-band could not even share the vulnerabilities because I would not show any of my own. I was not transparent, did not understand myself, and yet lay expectations on him. In my darker moments, I asked myself, "Did he just marry me to have fun? Did he stay married to me in order to have financial support during den-tal school?" I bought and kept the house, worked full-time, did everything he wanted and needed, kept quiet so he could study, did not entertain much at all.

Following Tom to Switzerland after my cancer experience was the most challenging decision I made. I left my doctors, family, friends, work, church, and all support and came to a country where none of the primary three languages were English. No wonder I went into clinical depression six weeks after arriving! I could not get out of bed for weeks on end, yet I received no medical or psychological support. My insurance was valid only in America, and there was no one to help me. Tom tried to cope with work, research, language, and me—it was exhausting, for sure.

Journal

May 6, 1990
Huemoz, Switzerland

More from L'Abri: Love Life Rules Lecture

Prepare for the marriage work knowing that God gives grace. Adultery = sin = forgiveness as of God. He must see in me a living, walking example of God's truth being faithfully applied.

Avoid separation. Make him glad to be there with you. Just accept him and use the time to grow in the Lord. Respond with love at every opportunity.

Prepare to be "perfect," knowing you have a sufficiency of grace. The Lord may have to change me first. I must do and be everything Scripture says. Consistently do everything you can to please your mate and meet their needs. Consistently show your mate respect and honor, whether he deserves it or not. Totally avoid criticism of your mate.

Prepare to be rejected, knowing you have a sufficiency of grace. Love is something we must work at and build. Don't ask for a kiss or to say "I love you."

Becoming Best Friends

Women:

1. Never repeat to anyone the things your husband shares privately.
2. Give your husband attention when he speaks.

3. Do not interrupt or expect that you understand what he means.
4. Acknowledge understanding even if you
   disagree.
5. When share thoughts, don't blame.

Men:

1. Spend time alone together.
2. Look at your wife and move closer to her.
3. Plan for times of uninterrupted attention.
4. Arrange for long times of sex.
5. Pay attention to your wife when others are
   around.

Choose with your will to love your mate
unconditionally and permanently through attitude, word, and action.

Saved husbands and wives are not always
obedient to the Word.

With these notes written and cried over, I left L'Abri to return
home to work more diligently on my marriage. I was completely
unaware at that time that my husband was with another man romantically in Cardiff, Wales.

Then when lust has conceived, it gives birth to sin; and when sin is accomplished, it brings forth death. Do not be deceived, my beloved brethren. (James 1:15–16, NASB)

Do not be deceived: "Bad company corrupts good morals." (1 Corinthians 15:33, NASB)

CHAPTER 9

CRAFTINESS:
RIDICULOUS BEGINNING

My written words seem ridiculous, knowing I wrote them in light of the impossibility of staying in the marriage. I did not know what I did not know. I believed that I could keep my husband in love with me and in the marriage by changing myself into what he wanted and needed. That was my hope and my goal, and I pursued it with hours of prayer and Bible Study, readings, and never telling anyone of our problems. As a Bible study leader, no one knew of my pain. My personal performance and Christian face were invaluable in the mutual deception.

People have asked me if I really believed my husband was a Christian. Absolutely. I would not have married him if he were not a Christian. He confessed Christ as his Savior and had followed Christ since he was a child. We had met at work, where we partied with a group of friends and became close, but neither of us was living a "Christian" life.

I was certainly not promiscuous, but there were men, lots of drinking, and wild parties with the medical students in Texas. My first few years after college, I ran as far from God as I could and still went to church on Sunday. Sometimes. When I worked as a medical technologist, we had to "shake" tubes in order to cross-match the blood and look for coagulation or not. I would be so shaky from drinking and lack of sleep that sometimes I just held up the tube and it shook without my effort. Not my proudest moments.

We were in a group of friends who went to gay bars on "Straight Thursday," straight bars, dancing, concerts, and private parties. When the medical students completed their finals, it was quite a scene, and the town was invited. My roommate and my future husband owned a catamaran together, and we would all sail together on the weekend. We sailed, drank, and hung over the edge of the catamaran with the dolphins, followed up with dinners of shrimp, oysters, and crabs. It was a wild couple of years, and then I fell in love.

My future husband was handsome, smart, funny, and sarcastic. He liked to party, but he was also a good one-on-one communicator. He remembered my long, long hair and my every finger covered with rings and no fingernails. The first time I met him in the employee lounge, I found him cute, thin, kind, and really energetic. After a year of engagement and wedding preparation, we were married in my hometown. Friends and family came from many states for the celebration the same summer that Princess Diana was married. We were educated, we had jobs, and we were a bit older and sure of our choices. We had to move our outdoor wedding into the church at the last minute due to rain. Years later, I wondered if that was a sign. We left for our honeymoon in Mexico and had a great start to our married life together.

Six months into our marriage, I sat on the stairs of our rented townhouse wondering if I had made a mistake. He was angry, drinking, and never sleeping a complete night in bed with me. We decided to get back into a church and start worshiping together. We found a new group of friends at church and support for our fledgling and struggling marriage. Couples became our friends, and as I finished graduate school and he applied for professional schools, we made decisions to move to the next phase of our lives together. Professional success waited, but it would be in another city.

And I will punish on that day all who leap on the temple threshold, who fill the house of their lord with violence and deceit. (Zephaniah 1:9, NASB)

CHAPTER 10
JUGGLING: REFUSE DIVORCE

My mind was a whirlwind of confusion and silence only punctuated by massive hysteria. God was revealing the truth to me, and I could not breathe. What may be "wrong" is so deceptive that my mind cannot grasp the thought. I finally asked him if he was "in love" with the Scottish guy he had met in England and who was visiting in Switzerland. He was acting like a teenager, whispering on the phone, waiting expectantly by the door of the apartment for his "friend" to visit and ignoring everyone and everything that did not revolve around this man. He asks for a divorce, and my panic and tumultuous bewilderment collide with the Bible.

Journal

June 20, 1990

I must have surgery on my toe for an ingrown toenail. Unbelievable pain for something so small, and I really thought I would hit the Swiss doctor who squeezed it at the hospital. I have never come close to physically punching someone, but after yelling at him, he did not touch me again. My friend says your toe is just like Christ, when He gets inside you, He affects every part of your life.

Journal

June 22, 1990

Toe surgery where I waited two hours and prayed to be able to speak enough German while I was alone. Medicine is adequate and the pain was not too bad. He went out with a friend from England after he brought me home from surgery.

Journal

June 24, 1990

My husband wants a divorce, and I am completely warm and surrounded by God's love. I asked him if he was having an affair with a guy he met in England, since they had been together every day for the last week. He called me a selfish bitch and said his friends think I am also. Who has he talked to?

There is a line of respect, and his selfishness has no bounds.

He stated something about not being with me if I could think that about him. I remember his harmful words that I was raised to be like a man and still act so, and if he was not selfish he would be swallowed up by my domination. He denied any relationship with his man friend and suggested that I was sick with jealousy.

I think he "doth protest too much." One week or more waiting for his anger to cool, so God has given me this time with Him—dependent, learning, immersing myself in prayer alone. God is with me—a warm presence. I had to ask.

What will happen? I do not know. His parents come in ten days for a visit. Does he want separate apartments? Does he want me to cancel the trip? Maybe his "friend" can go? No. It is also my money for this trip. Maybe this will be a goodbye anniversary trip?

Tomorrow is another day. "Lord, forgive me when my love is not patient or kind or forgiving and thank You for loving me unconditionally. I hate to keep coming to God for prayer and asking others what to do, because it is like crying wolf at the door. Or is it? Is it a dam slowly springing one leak, two leaks, until the foundation gives way and the flood overflows? I am beginning to question if I am married to a believer or follower of Christ—do I let him go?

Journal

June 25, 1990

When you do it alone, God will reward me for suffering for the "right" and working all things together for good, because I am called according to His purposes. The only time I asked.

Consider your options—The Lord has provided time through an injured foot operated on for ingrown toenail to do quiet, uninterrupted Bible Study and prayerfully consider God's plan for me.

"For nothing is impossible with God. I am the Lord's servant," Mary answered. (Luke 1:37–38, NIV)

Refuse divorce—know what God's word says.

You ask, "Why?" It is because the Lord is acting as the witness between you and the wife of your youth, because you have broken faith with her, though she is your partner, the wife of your marriage covenant. Has not the Lord made them one? In flesh and spirit they are his. And why one? Because he was seeking godly offspring. So guard yourself in your spirit, and do not break faith with the wife of your youth. "I hate divorce," says the Lord God of Israel, "and I hate a man's covering himself with violence as well as with his garment," says the Lord Almighty. So guard yourself in your spirit, and do not break faith. (Malachi 2:14–16, NIV)

It is God's will in every marriage for the couple to love each other and have an absorbing spiritual, emotional, and physical attraction that continues to grow throughout their lifetime. Marriage is sacred; I am bound to my husband no matter the outcome. I have to feel and know that I have done all I could. Do not listen to unbiblical counsel. Stabilize my emotions. I am in a highly nervous state being "fearful of losing my mind." I saw where I had to change my ways, and really only needed to talk about this to the Lord, not to people. "Fly by the best instrument." Steady my heart by God's word and fix my eyes intently on God.

My List after my husband told me he wanted a divorce.

1. Am I committed to this marriage?
2. Lord, will you meet my emotional needs?
3. Help me to give him warm acceptance.
4. Don't discuss marital problems widely outside of the marriage.
5. Choose biblical counselor wisely.

6. Spend as much time as possible in the Bible.
7. Focus on God and my mistakes, not his.
8. Do not separate.
9. Do not give a divorce.
10. Spend time with Encouragers.
11. Keep your mouth shut—be Christ like, don't defend yourself verbally.
12. Don't fall into old behavior patterns.

For I am afraid that when I come I may not find you as I want you to be, and you may not find me as you want me to be. I fear that there may be quarreling, jealousy, outbursts of anger, factions, slander, gossip, arrogance and disorder. I am afraid that when I come again my God will humble me before you, and I will be grieved over many who have sinned earlier and have not repented of the impurity, sexual sin and debauchery in which they have indulged. (2 Corinthians 12:20–21, NIV)

Journal

June 26, 1990

The only time I ever asked God to direct me to a scripture when I opened up the Bible, He graciously gave me an amazing scripture.

Do not be afraid; you will not suffer shame. Do not fear disgrace; you will not be humiliated. You will forget the shame of your youth and remember no more the reproach of your widowhood. For your Maker is your husband—the Lord Almighty is his name—the Holy One of Israel is your Redeemer; he is called the God of all the earth. The Lord will call you back as if you were a wife deserted and distressed in spirit—a wife who married young, only to be rejected," says your God. "For a brief moment I abandoned you, but with deep compassion I will bring you back. (Isaiah 54:4–7, NIV)

This most marvelous Scripture was given to me by God when my husband asked for a divorce.

Journal

June 27, 1990

And so it begins... A journey of separation and finding grace of God.

My husband says, "That is the cruelest, most vicious thing you could have said (about him being in love with a man), and I want you out now. I will not pretend with my parents during their visit. I don't care what you do; I just want no more talking, no arguing. Get out of here. Go stay with some of your Christian friends."

It was only words—harmful, devastating words to him. God has forgiven me for saying it, but can my husband? Who is the injured party here? I want to be accusing, but that doesn't show love. He hasn't gone out or called the Scottish guy the last two nights. Why? Why the abrupt change in behavior? Then I read of other people who are in such a bad position and I know it could be worse. A widowed mom with two or four kids, someone without friends or family, someone without faith, dying alone: it could be worse. Yes fifty per cent of the fault is mine, but if it hadn't been this conversation, it would have been something else. The pressures of responsibility were overwhelming to him and he wants to be free. So he is free to pursue his life in whatever way he chooses.

I listened to a tape about peace from our former Sunday School teacher in the States. The world longs for peace. Peace is an agreement to end hostilities or a state of calm. It is the freedom from disturbing thoughts and emotions. Peace is a cessation of hostilities by God. End of strife for man. A state of rest from within.

God created man to be at peace with Him with the understanding that God is God. You have no peace until you make peace with God. Surrender—no terms. "You know the message God sent to the people of Israel, telling the good news of peace through Jesus Christ, who is Lord of all" (Acts 10:36, NIV).

Man wants peace at any cost, and the Bible is full of verses about peace. Bless those who curse you. Pray for your enemies. Share joy and grief with someone. Do not be haughty or snobby to others who are over you. Don't think you are better—remember God died for you. Don't pay back evil with evil. Don't take your own revenge or retaliate. Give yourself to humble tasks. If possible, live at peace; be above reproach; do not always be challenging or confrontational.

Peace is a gift from God, from His Spirit, and is unrelated to our temperament. God's peace is totally different from the world. It is an order from God to not be troubled or afraid.

Peace I leave with you; my peace I give you. I do not give to you as the world gives. Do not let your hearts be troubled and do not be afraid. (John 14:27, NIV)

Journal

June 28, 1990

Joy is not happiness, nor is it a feeling or expression. Joy comes from our inner relationship with the Father. Try to see everything from God's eternal perspective. Who God was—word; What God says—worth; What God did—works; and How God did it—ways. My husband wants me out immediately.

"Consider it all joy when you encounter various trials, knowing that the testing of your faith produces endurance" (James 1:2, NASB).

We are not to endure trials; we are to rejoice in them.

Joy is a heart attitude that reflects excitement over things eternal. Joy is a supernatural inner expression of joy over part of God's nature. It is excitement and contentment released even more when we view life from God's circumstances. Pray for character, not happiness. Fill me with the Spirit of Joy!

Let my life be filled with your love. You and I, we've faced things together that I know I could not face alone. You stand firm in times when I am the weakest. And when I need you, I know you will be strong. So I give all that I am to you, nothing I withhold from you now. Come back into my life again. Live in my heart and let my days be filled with your love.

Only time will tell if we will stay together.
Though my, oh my love binds me to you.
We have shared so much and so deeply.
I know that to leave you will tear me apart.

Release the worries about the Bible study ladies, knowing that they will relate to you even more after they have seen that you also suffer and are not spiritually perfect or all together. Do you want to stay with him if things remain as they are? No, but I still love my husband.

Gather these ashes in your hands.
Lift them up and offer them to God.
He promised to give you beauty for ashes.
Give Him broken dreams.
Give Him broken relationships.

He will make something beautiful out of them and of your life. You will do to others what has been done to you unless you have been healed by Christ's wounds. Pray for binding Satan's effect of harmful words. See Christ in the center of healing memories. Meditate on Who God is! It brings you joy. When lonely, crawl into God's arms. God is on his throne and Satan is defeated.

Journal

June 30, 1990

Don't Leave.

I love him enough to let him go, to give him what he needs and he thinks he needs to be alone. If he were sick I wouldn't leave him. I must/will/shall/can not leave you or break this marriage commitment.

Perhaps I need to be strong and give him a "wall" to push against. Give God credit for his sense of humor and timing. My ingrown toe is so injured, I cannot "walk out." I went to Zurich to visit with a friend for some spiritual guidance.

Love is going toward someone with no sense of self-protection. I approach this not with set statements, but am open to pain and rejection and acknowledge my own confusion with apologies. He said, "You are a Bible 'addict' with no respect for him. I think he is an alcoholic and sleeps with men. What is there left in this relationship?" He said he doesn't love me, care for me, doesn't want harm to come to me, but does not care to ever see me again. He continues that I am not his ideal of a Christian woman and wife, but a Christian and very charismatic with people. Very painful.

Maybe I should be single for the Lord!

He continued, "You are using me because of your fear of being alone and coping with the real world. You were not able to take a job, so life cannot be enjoyed because of your pride." At least there is no screaming.

The issues are very complex, and I ask myself, "Am I using Bible study as a crutch to fulfill my emotional needs?" Jesus emptied himself—humbled himself in obedience to death with no regard for equality as something to be grasped. Reading Philippians 4 again and again. This is what it means to be a Christ follower. Pain of emptying yourself, no self-protection, regarding my husband as better than me and dying to myself, being obedient to the Word, and to love as shown in I Corinthians 13 in the Bible.

If you have ever faced divorce in your life, you understand the wrenching dichotomy of loss and gain of peace and joy. I was immersed in prayer and studying the scripture, and time passed during this most terrible time. In the early 1990s, there was no internet, no Skype, expensive international calls, and we lived in a foreign country with our money, and even passports, tied to Switzerland. I knew he had a bad temper, as I had been the recipient of outbursts before this time. His anger was volcanic eruptions spewing hate, showing hot red glowing eyes, and tossing hot burning coals on me. It was physically scary.

Yet in spite of all this her treacherous sister Judah did not return to Me with all her heart, but rather in deception," declares the Lord. (Jeremiah 3:10, NASB)

CHAPTER 11
SNOW JOB: ROLLERCOASTER REALITY

Problems in a marriage can be hidden from most people, as they are not in your home. Children can feel the issues and may even develop stress related symptoms to their parents fighting or concerns. This was one time I was thankful I had no children. I cannot even imagine the challenge of deception within the home with other people living with you.

We faced the task of his parents coming for their only European vacation with their only beloved son and his tolerated wife. I remember much later my family saying at the wedding, "Well, they are definitely interesting." I liked everyone in his family during our twelve-year marriage, and yet, I was not ever fully accepted into the family. There was a "doting on her son" mother-in-law and a father-in-law so proud of his doctor son, but Tom disliked and was even ashamed of them. I wonder what happened to them when we divorced. I never spoke to them again.

Journal

July 15, 1990

My husband's parents came for two weeks in July, a very challenging time for all of us. We went to Salzburg, Vienna, and Budapest. We saw where the movie Sound of Music was filmed and traveled to where my husband had been in college. Our time in Vienna was short, and all I remember was a castle and live music with coffee. His parents were challenging to travel with on their first trip outside of the United States. Budapest was filled with Gypsies, old World War II relics, museums, a marvelous concert, authentic Hungarian goulash, and a church with magnificent architecture.

We then traveled over the Alps all night on a train and arrived at beautiful, magical, romantic, fantastic Venice. Venice was different being with my husband. I had visited Venice with a friend before then. We left his parents to go to art museums and wander the city together but alone. In pictures from that trip, I look so very sad, and Tom looks defiant.

We watched the Opera "Carmen" in an ancient amphitheater in Verona. My toe was infected again after the surgery, and I looked everywhere for salt for footbaths. I did not want to go to the Italian hospital, so I was unable to walk very much. We were uncertain, on edge, sharing a bed without touching or breathing the same air. Tom's parents could feel the tension; they could see we were in trouble, and his mother admonished him to not speak to me like that. She had overheard him call me foul names as we walked down a street. I can still see the sidewalk, see him walking away from me with anger so palpable it shook the air. The tension of pretense was enormous.

When Tom's parents left Switzerland, he only remembered their comforting words and actions toward me. It made him furious. They drove him crazy as traveling partners, and everything we saw was tainted with this poison of ridiculous pretense.

Journal

July 26, 1990

He wants to walk with me and talk about leaving in October. Where do we go to live? Huh? We? What would be happening if I had left? I walked for two and half hours today. Can I forgive and forget?

Journal

August 3, 1990

We have talked about changes in the marriage or leaving Switzerland, how we both are at fault and that living in a foreign country has unique stress. Our relationship is healing slowly from this summer.

Journal

September 21, 1990

I was at retreat for Bible study in Liverpool and afterwards, went off by myself for some time in England. I had to visit Nottingham—the home of Snot and his party! Why Snot you may ask? We know he was called Snot because the "S" is seen in the early records and was dropped from the name during the Norman period. Snot in Old English meant, "wise." Now it means something very different.

Journal

September 24, 1990

Had a traditional tea at Ann and Malcolm's house and then visited the Liverpool Cathedral. I took a train to Stratford on Avon, Shakespeare's Home, and stayed at a charming bed and breakfast. The breakfast was bacon, tomatoes, and toast. It is so absolutely marvelous to be in an English speaking foreign country.

The visit had brought a change in direction. Did his parents say something to him? I knew his mother was shocked at how he treated and spoke to me. I was saying nothing, just preparing for the return to America, separating and moving on with my life. Abruptly, he wants to go back to America and try again at the marriage. This rollercoaster ride was crazy, but I was holding on to the hope that we would thrive in our marriage like you hold on to the sides of the rollercoaster seats as it climbs. Then you take the wild ride down the other side and through up you hands in the air. Screaming the whole way down.

Therefore, give orders for the grave to be made secure until the third day, otherwise His disciples may come and steal Him away and say to the people, "He has risen from the dead," and the last deception will be worse than the first. (Matthew 27:64, NASB)

CHAPTER 12
FRAUDULENT: RENEWAL IN AMERICA

Throughout that horrific summer, the pain of being together was worse than the pain of separating. We were in a foreign country with an apartment, jobs, and relationships. A switch was flipped after my husband's parents' visit, and he wanted to return together. I never knew if he saw the Englishman again, if he spoke with him, or if I was completely off base. I just went to work as did he, and we tried to stay out of each other's space. We both walked on eggshells as we tried to rebuild our marriage. Many people know what it's like to live with an alcoholic or rage-oholic. My pulse and breath accelerated from the tension every time Tom entered the apartment or the room. It is a miserable place to be, but you do survive it. Barely.

We had to decide either to stay in Switzerland for a much longer time for his profession or to return to America. I was hopeful after deciding to return to America. We would experience grief in leaving Switzerland and all our wonderful friends there. My Bible study leaders gave us a "goodbye" party at a castle in the French-speaking area. I received gifts of paintings, a finely cut paper picture (a Swiss specialty), and pottery. The church fondly bid us farewell, and Tom's work colleagues from the university provided closure through several parties and suppers.

We took one more trip together alone through Southern Germany and Bavaria. I wanted to see Castle Neuschwanstein, Oberammergau, and Dachau near Munich before I left Europe. We borrowed a car from some friends and left for a few days. We had always traveled well together, and fulfilling some of my travel wishes felt to me like a gift of reconciliation. Dachau concentration camp made us quiet and reflective. That suffering put mine in perspective as the spirits of those who had died cried out for peace.

Journal

December 20, 1990

I have fear of our relationship not surviving without any change. I have fear of my husband never coping better. I have fear of trying to mother him in lieu of a child. I have fear of his awful dark side resurfacing when there is stress again. I have fear of him feeling so low about himself for having no job, and that I must build him up. I have fear of being alone with him my entire life as he is—that is my greatest fear.

Why are all my thoughts and fears focused on him? Because he affects me, because we have become dysfunctional, not enough sex, too much alcohol, little joy, his boredom and unhappiness.

Maybe it is time for me to seek help again. I know money will be the issue, but isn't it better to seek help when things are not so explosive? I keep thinking about something someone said to me, "If you don't deal with these problems, they will return even stronger!" Maybe I am the coward so fearful of anger and conflict.

"If you are willing to serenely bear the trial of being displeasing to yourself, then you will be for Jesus a pleasant place of shelter," Saint Therese of Lisieux.

Journal

December 26, 1990

My husband asks God to do what He will in his life and is expecting miracles. He has looked for work for two months, as have I. There was just that one sentence from him that he was asking God for help. He bought a commentary to help him study the New Testament. I am thrilled by his interest in God's word, but cautious. It is time for prayer.

We decided to return to America together in October, over three years after my cancer and thirty-two months after moving to Switzerland. We landed in Chicago, Illinois, and rented a car to go to visit my parents. We bought a car from my parents and left there after only two days, even though we had not seen them for almost two years. We had been gone from America almost three years, but Tom could not stand being around my family. We spent the rest of that year re-establishing a home in America, re-adapting to all the changes in culture, and renewing relationships all over Texas.

We looked for work in Texas, found a place to live, and re-adjusted to the culture of America. It was tense, but we were on the same team for a time.

Do not be deceived, God is not mocked;
for whatever a man sows, this he will also reap.
(Galatians 6:7, NASB)

CHAPTER 13
DUPLICITY: RELUCTANCE

We found a townhouse in a central location near the medical center. I reconnected with my marketing colleagues and found a great job establishing a call center and doing physician marketing for a hospital. My husband found a position with a dentist who was expanding his practice by having office hours in the evenings. We went to church and exercised frequently. We read books, ate out, cooked at home, traveled, and had a normal married life, including sex.

My best friends had conceived children while I was away in Switzerland, and I was able to share in their young children's lives. Even though I still did not have my heart's desires (a house, children, and a dog), I had learned to be content. Readjustment to America was extensive: food, shopping, money, ministry, and language. It was as much of a culture shock to return to America as it had been three years before when we moved to Switzerland. All the pop culture and sport references people made were lost on both of us. Life was good.

Depression seeped in and became our constant companion, especially for my husband. We knew he needed counseling. I helped start a new Bible study on the south side of town and was teaching regularly. Church was going well and we were active in Sunday school classes. But something was under the surface, hovering in our spirits, and it felt like a huge dark bear waiting to attack. It did.

Journal

April 8, 1992

Sixteen Months Later

It begins again—the anger, the tears, the cursing, the hate, and I am too emotionally tired to cope again. I called my husband's therapist today to find some help in books. Workaholic and Anger books—that's for me.

He was furious that I had called and told me to "get my own damn therapist." I have cried the last two days and told him Sunday, "Why don't you just kill yourself if you are so miserable?" Mean, cold, and exactly how I feel. He is furious and cannot forgive me for these words. So now... What will I have to add to words from two years ago? Lord, what is wisdom in fire?

Three months later, in July 1992, I am alone. I have no husband. I have no children. My greatest fear has become real: I am alone. As the new normal settled into my being, I took a vacation. Tom and I had planned to go to Idaho to hike and visit my friends from Zurich that fall. Suddenly, I had to go alone. Money issues? Yes, but so what. Depression? It will follow me there. I have to adjust to the new normal in the only way I know how. Hike. I trained for two months until I was walking up a thousand steps on the Stairmaster and two hundred steps backward. I was going to a place where I would be hiking alone for four to six miles a day and staying in a rustic cabin at night.

No matter what causes you to be alone after a long time with a partner, it is a shock to the system. The person who shared the planning, the pleasure, and the responsibility is gone from your life. It is all up to you. I was a college-educated world traveler, and this vacation caused my stomach to roll. I had an apartment, a bank account, a therapist, and a job, so I was more fortunate than others in the same circumstance. I did not have kids, so I was spared the complication of those issues common in so many separations or divorces.

I felt as if my arm had been cut off but was still attached and hanging there. Grief, anger, denial, and giddiness made regular excursions into my consciousness. I was functioning, not functional. I was dead inside and in great need of affection. I was vulnerable to any man who was nice to me. I was looking for love while processing the loss of love through my journal and my letters. It was not pretty. I won my second survivor badge: I had one for cancer and one for divorce.

For weeks, I constantly played Bonnie Raitt's "I Can't Make You Love Me if You Don't."

Journal

August 31, 1992

Thoughts:

1. When my husband looks at me, he sees his shame and his guilt because he cannot do what is being required of him—affirm my womanhood.
2. People overcome problems like this all the time—but they must seek help.
3. The "problem" is about him and his issues—not just me.
4. As I affirm my femininity, I will no longer be afraid of him, but will talk strongly and firmly with boundaries.

5. He will seek help or he will get worse. What is worse? Choose to be gay?
6. My feelings of rejection are very real. If my husband had to choose right now—he might choose a guy over being with me.

Journal

September 1, 1992

Vacation alone in Idaho

No people, but whoever is there, they are friendly. I can see the Sawtooth Mountains as I leave Boise and the devastation of the forest fires. I turned off the radio and just drove in the silence of the wind through the windows. There was an incredible darkness and stillness as I went further into the mountains. I had a brief thought about being hurt by a bear—I am alone—whom would I call to help me? Not my husband.

The plane delay meant twelve hours of travel, not a great first day of vacation. I am wired and have to be doing something all the time. There are places to river raft and horseback ride here. I am nervous about money. Do I have enough? I spent $25 on food at the grocery store and will not eat out, but how long will that last me? I seem to have to force the stillness. I was screaming and singing in the car I was so excited to be doing this trip. I am alone. I have thought about my death dream…there is a mountain lake and the car goes into it, and the children drown. But I don't have children.

I am luxuriating in the fall colors of Idaho. Two years ago I was in England at this time, and three years ago I was in Southern Switzerland in the Ticino Region. There is wildness to the woods, dry, and no lush wetness. The air is cool in the morning, and I watch the sunset and moonrise from my balcony. How do I change myself to find something pleasurable and joyful every day?

I hiked to Lake Sawtooth, eleven miles round-trip alone. I fed the chipmunks, sat in the warm sun, had a beer with my lunch, and shared it with a distracting young man. The Sawtooth Mountains look like a mini-Eiger, Monch, Jungfrau of the Bernese Oberland near my Switzerland home with their sharp spikes. The next day I hiked to Bench Lakes above Red Fish, only about 6 miles round trip. It was a difficult rocky terrain with yellow Aspen. The Elk were in the distance refreshing themselves at Lake Stanley. I walk every day and cry every night. My grief is occurring, and I am observing it and healing by reading a romantic novel.

Journal

September 5, 1992

I hiked up the West Mountain overlooking the town of Cascade, Idaho, and the Reservoir. I walked in anger and cried, but still I cannot voice the anger. I screamed into my pillow last night—I am not you, I am me! The pain of the grief of disappointing my parents makes me physically ill. I could not sleep for a long time, and I think it is time to write letters to my parents.

Journal

September 7, 1992

I went white water rafting on the Cascade River—it is a roller coaster, then it is like a rocking horse. Physically exhilarating, scary but fun, FUN! How long has it been since I have had fun? The highlight is the girl who falls overboard, and is riding along with us in the river until we can get to a calm spot and pull her into the boat. Our guides were very experienced, the meal was excellent, a quiet river with osprey swooping and trees, always trees. Seeing and hearing white water and trying to tuck your feet under the ballasts to stay in the seat on your roller coaster—hang on toes. "My self-preservation streak is very strong," says our guide Steve Jones.

That is the way I feel now—STRONG— what can mere man do to me? Thank you God for this time, the people not here and the ones I meet, and your creation. I am alone for one whole week. This will always be a healing place for me: Cascade Raft Company, Garden Valley, Idaho. The name says it all.

Journal

September 14, 1992

Patient Passion

To be able to spend time
Alone, Together.
Not limited by commitments
Desired, Treasured.

It will be precious, intense
Later, if ever.
To be able to only stare
At the object of desire.

Put away the distractions
Self-control, others.
Allow wholeness, fullness
Passion in patience

Passion in Patience. The man who helped me to feel human and female again was unavailable because he was my boss.

I shared my letter I had written to him in Idaho after a meeting. He was surprised and delighted. No one had given him a gift like that before and that was how he viewed it. He clued in on the "romantic fantasy" part. He thought I was giving him a letter of resignation and telling him how stupid the job is.

I told him about the depth of my healing that was required, about my negative test regarding exposure to HIV, but not until he had read my letter. He is surprised. I make him laugh. No one had ever asked questions about his wife and her death before. He has shared things with me that he has not shared with anyone. But I am vulnerable right now. The attraction is mutual and he asked to keep the letter. He ripped it out of my journal.

We may explore the feelings in the future, if and when I have healed and resolved how I am to live. Had I noticed he was attracted to me? Yes. It was a wonderful intimate two and one half hour conversation. And nothing can change; yet everything changes. My heart was warmed all night and

I floated the next day. The sight of him and the sound of his voice, and I am like a teenager in my heart. A touch and I am sure I will become flushed. I am now constantly listening to Bonnie Raitt's song, "Let's Give Them Something to Talk About"

But evil men and impostors will proceed from bad to worse, deceiving and being deceived. (2 Timothy 3:13, NASB)

CHAPTER 14
EQUIVOCATION: REQUISITE GRIEF

When I returned from Idaho, I was different. I had hiked alone, cried and screamed into the wilderness, and grieved my old life. I do not think anyone can force the timing of this process. Grief moves through your world of color to become black and white with shades of gray. I had a flicker of hope for another relationship, but it was much too early in my recovery process. God continued to comfort me through people, the Bible, and my journal. I knew that life as I had known it for over twelve years had ended, but I had no idea what pain still awaited me.

God is the God of all comfort, but God is a jealous God and will have no other gods before Him. Every piece of my identity was about to be removed so that He could remake me. A sledgehammer smashed all of my identities. The losses multiplied, swamped my very breath, and broke my spirit.

Journal

September 17, 1992

I awoke from a dream in the early morning in tremendous emotional pain. There were four babies available and couples were waiting for them. My husband was there with our best friends, and our friends from Switzerland were waiting as well. I was there alone. I finally could not take the pain of waiting and went to a table and sat and cried with two other people. The weather changed and it started to rain. We three ran to the building where all the couples were competing for babies. My husband and our friends came to pay for their baby. The two babies had played with me, smiled and cooed. They were not cute. I was in such pain; I had to know how much my husband would have to pay for a baby with someone else. I walked to the table to ask him, and tried to see how much the check was for. I felt total rejection. I want to avoid any quiet time and dealing with these processes.

Journal

September 18, 1992

Malcolm Smith Ministries gave a two night lecture series and I bought his book "Heal My Hurts." The following was some of the lessons I learned in that changing time. Deep necessary healing was happening, and with God's help, I was led to the right places and people at the time I needed them.

Unconditional love—the lie Satan has fooled us with is that we can be gods, perfect—and when we fail in those areas of importance, our failure causes us to have negative self-worth.

Anger can come toward those whose expectations we cannot fulfill. Many men who are effeminate cannot be the man their parents and wife wanted. In their anger and frustration, they turn to the same sex for love and acceptance instead of turning to God.

Anger can come from being embarrassed from our association with others. Many women turn away from their mates or divorce them because they are reacting to pent-up anger. They have been humiliated or embarrassed for years by their mate.

Grace plus love equals the power to change.

1. Iniquities of fathers visited on third and fourth generations of those who hate me (from Exodus).

2. When we sin, we are affecting others and ourselves. Sin in a family bends and twists them to iniquities in the future.

3. I am a result of all my choices, and that is based on the choices of my parents and then of their parents.

4. Adam and Eve are removed from the Garden and have a deep sense of shame that they pass on to all in reaction to the lies they believed.

5. Parents are responsible for what they did or did not do. It is between them and God. I am responsible only for what I do with the pain they cause me.

6. As a child, we cannot edit parental comments. We have complete belief in what they say, whether it is perceived or real.

7. As a child, we manipulate and control our parents in order to get the love we need.

8. Abuse builds into us shame and a sense of rejection. Whether it is from being abandoned or adopted, the death of a parent, or a workaholic or absent parent. They may be physically present but emotionally absent.

9. Verbal abuse is when nothing is said that is positive. The comments are always critical.

"You will never amount to anything. After all we sacrificed for you… You should have been a boy/girl…what will the family and neighbors say? God will not love you if you are naughty."

10. Religious abuse in the home looks like performance in order to earn approval. No mercy for failures. Despise everyone who is not like you or does not worship like you.

11. Grief, sorrow, and shame of childhood may cause you to spend your life hiding the shame of your childhood. How can we have a relationship with an adult and cannot tell them everything? We react against adult abuse with rage and pain.

12. Victim Mentality by choice. We substitute importance and significance for the love we so desperately seek.

13. Abused people want love obsessively because of the emptiness they cannot show for fear of rejection again. When the parents stop abusing the person, the person takes over the abuse and repeats the same mistakes if there is no healing.

14. Abused people collect "important" friends or relationships in order to feel significant.

Jesus came to bind up the brokenhearted. Jesus comes to give the weary and heavy-laden rest.

Isaiah 53 in the Bible says that he "bore our grief and carries our sorrows, and the iniquity of us all fell upon Him."

Grief—weakness, distress, heartache, mourning and misery. Sorrow—pain of mind, 'If only…" hurt by someone else. Iniquities—Jesus carried our sins.

Death of Jesus was not painless like a lamb. He died bearing our grief and sorrows in his body. Judas betrayed him. How could he not know? Judas who continually kissed him revealed it in the Upper Room. John betrayed Jesus with silence. Peter betrayed Jesus with words.

The soldiers physically abused Jesus. Jesus was sexually abused in that he hung naked before even his mother to see. Jesus refused to drink myrrh as a narcotic so he could take the pain upon himself.

Our past is unchangeable, but Jesus takes out of it the grief and sorrow. My history has no lasting effect, and stands as a monument to God's grace. The Holy Spirit is the connection now between Jesus and us. My part is to tell the Holy Spirit, and let it out with my words. The Holy Spirit takes the garbage of my life and then puts it on Jesus' cross, and the grief can be gone forever. Jesus knows my pain of divorce, betrayal, loss of a child, and agony.

We are looking for the love of God whether in the refrigerator, shopping, sex or compulsions. God is calling me out of denial to come into the light. Calling me to tell the truth. To stop blaming or acting like a victim. I must face the fear of being alone forever and stop clinging to someone because I believe I am not worthy of being loved.

If I act like an Eve-type in the Garden, I will be quiet, take the blame of my spouse, grovel in the shame, and then accept the punishment. I will try to appease my mate. I will try to appease my husband by being a victim of Satan. No matter what my spouse does to me, even if they abuse me, I will remain the victim.

If the spouse acts like an Adam-type in the Garden, I will have no shame, and I will deny any weaknesses. I will show a compulsion to control every detail of my life and others. I will become a workaholic with total responsibility for everyone's happiness. I will try to solve everyone's problems so that someone will need me. I will be drawn to performance and hate the grace of God. I will live listening to the message, "What do you think of me?" I will despise imperfection in others and myself and point out other's faults. I will lash out at them in anger and then feel somewhat better and cleansed…at least for a short while.

Then Eve-type and Adam-type get together. Both are in a relationship to get love and are incapable of giving love, because they are manipulating, being deceitful and performing. This is Toxic Love. Until the couple faces their own issues separately, they will continue to try to control the other's issues.

If someone needs me to care for them, I will hide and deny anything that is unlovable. The real truth is so painful. I am not enough to love this person without God's strength. Denial birthed in the womb of fear says, "I want you to love me so badly, I will not show you the truth of myself for fear of your rejection." God allows us to come before him without pretense, without any shame or guilt. He has removed the condemnation for those of us who believe in Christ Jesus.

God created us with the need for love, but only God can fill the hole inside us with limitless and unconditional love. If I set my view on myself to fill my love need or on others to fill it, it is a demand that no one person or multiple people can fill. We will suck out of each other what little love there is, or is not there. We will manipulate others as a poor creature seeking someone to say nice things to me. Then we become dependent on each other, and not on God. This will never satisfy us.

I do not know what love is so I must say; "Come, Holy Spirit teach me."

I do not need you anymore, so I can say; "Now I can love you."

"Bless the Lord, who reigns in beauty. Bless the Lord who reigns in wisdom and with power. Bless the Lord who reigns in my life with so much love, He can make a perfect heart." This is a song I sang often during this healing heart time.

A.W. Tozer says, "God is vastly wonderful that He can meet those mysterious and deep needs no matter how deep and mysterious those needs are in me."

Journal

September 19, 1992

Wow! Unbelievable! Instantaneous! Grace! Unconditional Love! The Cross! Jesus an Abused Savior! Jesus bearing sorrow, grief, and iniquities! Jesus saying; "What things?" The Holy Spirit takes them to the Cross! My past is the same without grief or sorrow!

The pain was worth that miraculous spontaneous healing. All I had wanted was for my husband to love me—unconditionally. Only God could do that. He could not reveal himself to me for fear of rejection, guilt, and shame. We are both responsible for breaking the cycle and healing. The cycle cannot continue if we are to survive individually or separately.

I cannot go from one relationship to another, as has been my cycle. I must be whole ALONE with God, without a man. Jesus, be the lover of my Soul.

My husband is making no contact or effort to end the relationship. It is just "on hold" out there. People think I have great courage, am strong, but I want to collapse into the support of someone. I am plagued with "what ifs."

I came home from the Malcolm Smith conference and had a vision. I sat in my one-bedroom apartment in the one armless chair I had taken from the marriage home, and I wept. My hands lay limply on my lap, and I had no energy to get something to mop up my falling tears. Sobs wracked my body, and yet I could not move. I felt the presence of a "holy being" in the room with me. In my grief. In my sorrow. I looked at my hands and there were red marks in my palms. Wet with my tears, the centers of my palms were red. I cried out: "Jesus. In your suffering. In you taking all the sins, I have identified with you in your abuse. You have identified with me in my grief, sorrows, and iniquities. Jesus. You are real. You sent your Holy Spirit to comfort me with Your presence. Thank you." I slept for many unbroken hours for the first time in months.

The arrogance of your heart has deceived you, You who live in the clefts of the rock, In the loftiness of your dwelling place, Who say in your heart, "Who will bring me down to earth?" (Obadiah 3, NASB)

CHAPTER 15

DOUBLE-DEALING: REVELATION

Why did this happen? What did I not know? How can I never make a mistake like this again? The questions swirled in my head, blocking out all rational thinking. I was wise at 24, or so I thought. I had married a Christian, or at least one born into and raised in a Christian family, and willing to go to church and live by Christ's standards. He was a fun companion and we enjoyed doing many of the same things. The depth of deception was endless. My focus was on understanding the reasons why I chose him as my marriage partner, why I stayed when it was so bad, and how was I going to heal from this trauma. I made lists of what I needed, lists of what I had done wrong, and lists of what I learned from reading during this time. Would these lists really help me heal? I had no other choice.

Journal

September 23, 1992

From the Book: *Love is a Choice* by Minirth Meier

I don't know how to think positively about myself.
I cannot believe what others say about me, even the positive feedback.
My 'men' image is really messed up.

My whole life has been spent trying to keep everyone else happy.

I doubt my right to that same degree of happiness. Even just a little bit. Every big thing that I think will make me happy is unattainable: baby, love, marriage, relationship, no fear, health, and intimacy.

It is harder than I thought it would be to act normal after I shared my feelings with my boss. I am so proud of him. His words, how he acts is very admirable. I think there are things to change within me—but why? Do I have the need to see his eyes seek mine? Is it just a passing glance?

I know last week, he floated throughout the week and was happy and did see me. Now the emotions are more under control. We have a retreat to organize and put on with Dr. Paul Brand. The retreat meant much visual contact but very little talking to each other.

Am I acting weird? I have to quit my job here and must plan for this. Would I divorce if I did not have someone else interested in me? Yes. Why and what am I waiting for? When will it be the right time? How do I just put my life on hold? My husband is making no contact or effort to end the relationship.

Journal

September 26, 1992

My own pattern of emotional and verbal abuse is identified:

• Feeling anxious and nervous about approval of others

- Communicating my insecurities to the abuser
- Triggering the "deserved" abuse
- Feeling relief when "it" happened because it is familiar
- Being drawn to relationships as co-dependent
- Cannot identify healthy people in order to pattern behaviors

Journal

September 27, 1992

Loneliness

Quiet, Quietly waiting
Marking Time
Enjoying or Grieving?
To make my home and myself
Important to God.
To thank God for this time
To thank friends for their support.
To wait for God's timing
Again. Not to hurry. Again.

There are a few things I know I will not do again at the beginning of a relationship.

1. I will not have sex before marriage.
2. I will not lose friendship over having sex with a man.
3. I will pray for strength and self-control over physical desires.
4. I will wait for the man to pursue me.
5. I will wait upon God's timing and person.
6. I will not cling or need someone.

7. I will be whole before I re-open myself to relationships, no matter how difficult it is or how long.
8. I will remain in God's will daily, minute by minute.
9. I will not be ruled by my lust or need for love.
10. I will have pre-marital counseling and read many books together about relationships and romance.

That is why I am suffering as I am. Yet this is no cause for shame, because I know whom I have believed, and am convinced that he is able to guard what I have entrusted to him until that day. What you heard from me, keep as the pattern of sound teaching, with faith and love in Christ Jesus. (2 Timothy 1:12–14, NIV)

My Notes from book: *Grace Awakening* by Charles Swindoll

Grace releases and affirms.
Grace values dignity of individuals.
Grace supports and encourages.
Generosity—absence of selfishness
Encouragement—absence of predictability
Life beyond legalism—absence of Bible bashing of others
Creativity in faith—absence of expectations
Release from past—absence of shame

Guard the good deposit that was entrusted to you—guard it with the help of the Holy Spirit who lives in us.
I lost my best friend when my husband left me. We were friends before we were lovers, but there was no grace in my marriage. We live by encour-

agement and we die without it slowly, sadly, and angrily. What is grace in a marriage? What is grace outside of a marriage? I did not know.

Five needs of Woman

1. Affection—be loved and cherished
2. Conversation and companionship
3. Honesty and Openness
4. Financial support
5. Family Commitment

Five needs of Men

1. Sexual Fulfillment
2. Recreational
3. An attractive spouse
4. Domestic support
5. Admiration and respect

Journal

October 4, 1992

I called my husband and suggested we get together and talk.

He said: "Why?"

I want to share things I have learned from therapy and to discuss where do we go from here.

He said: "What issues?"

I said," You have made your wishes known from your letters, so we need to discuss it."

He said he would be gone this week and has company coming next weekend, so maybe we can talk in two weeks. I asked him to call me at work. He said for me to call him in two weeks.

Total indifference. Just do it!

Jim, a church counselor, said he is meeting with my husband weekly. Jim said that my husband would not discuss the issue, the marriage, or me; it is only superficial. He is being very religious to Jim saying; "what the Lord is doing in his life." My options for reconciliation are closing.

Journal

October 10, 1992

At Canyon Lake in the middle of Texas I was listening to a Bernie Siegel Meditation tape from my cancer year. As I came to my inner self—my body was tight and disconnected. Bernie asks us to play as if we are children and on the playground. I am always holding onto someone's adult hand. Then I walked into the lake (in my mind) nude and into healing water and minerals. I am up to my neck allowing the water to heal me.

Bernie Siegel asks us to look into the lake and find a healing message. My message caused me to start crying for real. Wholeness, being completely well. I then left the lake and lay on the shore alone, allowing the shame, the breast cancer and the body pain to flow out and be replaced with healing.

Bernie next asks us to go to an auditorium where all the significant people in your life are gathered to hear me perform. I chose to put on no makeup. I first thought I would sing a song to them about God's and my unconditional love to them. But then I sat down on the stage and did NOTHING. I would not perform for them anymore. I just sat there on the stage, loved them, and asked them to love me. Just as I was—not doing anything to please them—just love me as myself.

I took this meditation exercise to mean I was giving myself permission to divorce my gay husband. I realized I would be seen as a failure to the church, to God, my vows, my husband, my family, Bible study, and all our friends. But I am doing it for me to survive. It is what I have to do. It is what I want to do. Does that mean I am selfish? Maybe. But it is the only thing I want—to no longer be tied to this very ill, mean, and sad person.

I will be happier alone, even the rest of my life, than living in fear, nervousness, and anxiety.

Finally I believe I am worth being alive.

Reflection on this meditation experience: Patience and self-control are gifts of the Holy Spirit. God will tell me when it is time to move to a new location or a job. I only do work, but my boss wants to just talk. Family issues, weekend plans to visit Enchanted Rock.

"You have tried!" my boss says to me. Now my self-control weakens and I call him to say goodbye for the weekend. We touch hands as we part. Oh, to have hours together, but it is not to be.

Is it my place to hope for a remarriage someday? My understanding is that unless fornication of my husband is proven and he abandons me, I must remain unmarried as I am married to him in God's sight.

Journal

October 14, 1992

There will be no sleep tonight as I drank coffee at 8:30 p.m. at the Physicians St. Luke's evening with Paul Brand. How do I make a break from the hospital? In the last few days, friends from Switzerland called and said "Come, and we will help heal you and minister to you as you have done for us." I will call my husband and agree to end the marriage.

Journal

October 16, 1992

Dr. Paul Brand had many stories for the clergy. "When your life changes, it is because you become part of other's pain," he says.

I believe I must break from work, San Antonio, and my job in order to complete the healing. Is this a time to build a male friendship without intimacy? But our conversation is so intense—I am strangely turned on. I believe that my boss feels I am too vulnerable and fragile during this time of change. Strange, I feel stronger with less flowing motion daily. My vulnerability has allowed people to relate and share their sufferings. My boss cautions me to not always be with other wounded people. The happy and healthy need to be my "people" models.

Sometimes the healing comes in one side, but it is sucked away by the needy people in the world. Aloneness is to be cherished, not seen as isolation. The tendency to withdraw during this pain must be tempered with reaching out. These are wise words, but they are countered with the counselor's distancing words.

Six months from now, I will see Switzerland in bloom five years after I arrived there.

Journal

October 17, 1992

I am not sure why I have all the tears flowing today. So quiet, so alone. I am not connecting with anyone intimately. Touching only comes through healing massages. I need to be touched.

Switzerland—a place of healing. And yet it will be so full of the memories of my husband. I missed him terribly today. Lord, remind me why I left? I almost went to see him today. What is it that I need to be healed of internally? To be desired of no one and no thing—to be content to be where I am. I seem to be living so temporarily. Never cleaning, never moving in, never finishing things. That is I, and I will be comfortable with me someday. Not to fill the love need with food or shopping or sex. Just You. Oh, God. To make it without crying daily? But why?

I tried again to be reconciled to my husband or, at least, be civil. His rejection of this approach was a punch to my gut again. Visualization and dreams were documented as a way to work through the issues alone and with a therapist. I grasped at any lifeline of wisdom during this time—books, speakers, and friends. This was a time when I no longer trusted myself to make any decisions, and when I was stuck in this place, any movement seems impossible. I needed to be validated and loved by someone so badly when I now know that validation of my femininity and value as a human being can only come from God. Staying alone seemed impossible, and yet, staying alone was the only healing place.

Faithful are the wounds of a friend, But deceitful are the kisses of an enemy. (Proverbs 27:6, NASB)

CHAPTER 16
HYPOCRISY: REJECTION

Tom became the enemy. A once loving, trusting, and confiding relationship shifted to letters, lawyers, and hiding. I tell others that getting married is all about love and attraction; getting divorced is about property, money, pensions, jewelry, art, pets, and kids. A mistake many people make in divorce is giving in to whatever demands are made so they can "get out" of the marriage and the pain. Making this mistake is costly to many people in the long run. We have to walk through this pain and use attorneys or friends to stabilize us when our emotions scream, "Let me out."

Journal

October 23, 1992

The pain continues to intensify. Rejection is complete. I had the snake dream again where the room is full of poisonous snakes. If I lean over, they come off my long curly hair—which I don't have. It is a white room with a corner. My husband is asleep in the corner. I roll over onto my head and with my feet in the air, I ask my husband to wake up and help me repeatedly. There is a poised cobra at my left cheek. I keep begging him to wake up, stand up, and he struggles to awaken and I see him failing. I wake up just before the snake bites me.

I am doing everything I can. I am literally standing on my head—backed into a corner, begging my husband to wake up! Help me here! Snakes as phallic symbols? I walk through them unharmed.

I get another letter from my husband and he is giving me a two-week pre-notification of his intent to file divorce proceedings. He does not want to see me; we will do everything by mail or phone. After 13 years together—we have not spoken in person since I found out he may be gay.

My feeling of rejection was so strong and painful. I found a friend and went to the chapel at the hospital and just cried and cried. The finality. The pain. Over and over. Waves of hurt and sadness.

My friend Ginny said, "If you weren't grieving, I would be scared that you were hardening your heart."

My husband has hardened his heart. Our mutual hairdresser said he is so unhappy, but apparently not enough to change. She shocked me when she said she had seen him at a gay bar she frequents. Confirmation?

I meet with Clarence my attorney and he advises me to contact my husband by saying I will sign a waiver if he will file. Then we must settle our property through our attorneys. Divorce is hard and expensive. Money is just flowing out. Lord, please protect me.

I was serving as the leader for Bible study, because the main leader was sick from liver cancer. I called her and the people in charge of the Bible study to tell them my husband and I were going to separate, and that my husband was filing divorce papers. She said she was relieved it was he, not me filing.

The regional leader asked me not to come and be with the leaders the next morning as I was "not serving any good purpose by being there, and I certainly could not teach anymore."

I cried and cried on the phone with her. Nine years of my time, sacrifice, and attention to this group Bible study equaled rejection. It almost killed me, and suicide entered my thoughts.

My leader, Flo, disagrees with the decision. I told them I had been living separately from my husband since July and that he had notified me of his intent to file for divorce. Therefore, I am resigning from Bible study. Final blow. No good-bye. No thank you. No closure. Thank you very much Christians for your lack of support.

The feelings of rejection, worthlessness, abandonment, aloneness, and unreality are overpowering me. I feel a sense of depression and dark desperation that is not healthy. I wail from the depths of my soul. I desire the anesthesia of drunkenness.

This was the darkest moment of all. God was with me as I was stripped of all my identities that week. Spiritual leader, teacher, loyal soldier, wife, potential mother, failure as a daughter and godly woman: all my identities were gone. Jesus teaches us that we will identify with Him in our sufferings, that we will "take up His cross" as His disciples. All that I had learned about myself, and the mystifying reasons the marriage would ultimately fail was not enough. Suicide and drunkenness was what I craved as the pain descended upon me. I saw evil sitting in the corner of the room laughing. I saw Jesus as a spot of light in this darkness. My identification with Christ was complete. "My God, My God, why have You forsaken me?"

Bridge

It is over.
Is this the bridge?
Or my road?
When does the pain stop?
Healing me?

It is beginning.
Are the choices mine?
Or still others?
How do I start anew?
Healing again?

I don't want to fall
In love – I want to stand.
Even amid the barriers
Seeing Him clearly.

Journal

October 24, 1992

Notes from "The Applause of Heaven" by Max Lucado

Stubborn joy begins by breathing deep up there before you go crazy down here!
Before Christ went to the people, he went to the mountain.

Delight is one decision away—seize it. Go to a sacred summit. A place of permanence in a world of transition.

We're in need—poor in Spirit.

We repent of self-sufficiency—we mourn.

We surrender control to God—we're meek.

We yearn for his presence—we hunger and thirst.

We forgive others—we're merciful.

We change our outlook—we're pure in heart.

We love others—we're peacemakers.

We endure injustice—we're persecuted.

As long as Jesus is one of many options— He is no option.

As long as you can carry your burdens alone, you don't need a burden bearer.

As long as your situation brings you no grief, you will receive no comfort.

When there is truly no other name that you can call, then cast all your cares on Him, for he is waiting in the midst of the storm.

Deliriously joyful are the ones who believe that if God has used sticks, rocks, and spit to do His will, and then He can use us.

There is a Father who is ready to comfort me. There is a Father who will hold me until I am better, help me until I can live with the hurt, and who won't go to sleep when I'm afraid of waking up and seeing the dark. Ever. And that is enough.

I am crying hysterically at 5:00 a.m. when I normally would get up for Bible study meeting. Then finally calmness, peace, and sleep come over me. I am no longer viewed as a wife, a woman, a Christian. Who or what is left?

As a result, we are no longer to be children, tossed here and there by waves and carried about by every wind of doctrine, by the trickery of men, by craftiness in deceitful scheming, but speaking the truth in love, we are to grow up in all aspects into Him who is the head, even Christ. (Ephesians 4:14, NASB)

CHAPTER 17
UNTRUTH TO TRUTH: RELEASED

Release your fist. Whatever you are holding tightly to will be taken away if you idolize it more than you love God. All my fingers were pried open in one week, and I was left with open hands. Scarred, nail imprints, and scabbed, but open. Everything that I loved, that gave me identity, and that I was proud of was gone. In one week. He finally filed for divorce after my three months of silence. I will no longer be a wife and may never be a mother.

The Bible study group loss was almost as great as losing my husband. We are not allowed to teach if we are divorced. I would no longer be able to teach adult women the Bible. That was very hard to give up. The timing was such that I did not know when it would be over. I was rejected and alone, and my major reasons for living were gone. This was, and has remained, the lowest point in my life. Life was too difficult, too painful, and I considered ways to wreck my car or drink myself to oblivion.

The times when you want to drink yourself to unconsciousness or end your life are when you need true friends who are "God with skin." Flo was that friend to me. She was an older lady who was a mentor to me in life and in the Lord. She was a Bible study leader, had had cancer two times, and was facing her final cancer battle. The night I moved into my own apartment and had been kicked out of Bible study leadership because of my pending divorce, she showed up at my door with her husband Bob. She had battled alcohol and considered herself a recovering alcoholic, but because she had never been divorced, she was still in leadership. I had left a cruel bisexual husband for my own protection and was kicked out as a teacher. I was no longer a wife, a woman, and a Bible study leader, and I wanted to end my life. She quoted Zechariah 8:13 (NASB) to me. "I will save you that you may become a blessing. Do not fear; let your hands be strong."

God brought her to me, and when Flo left knowing that I was no longer suicidal, Jesus came to be with me and truly take my fears. His presence in the room during my tears and my screaming were real, and I felt His arms around me when I was so alone. My family lived many states away, and even though they were there for me by phone and prayers, that night, He brought me Flo. She pushed her way into the room, brought Bob with her, and they just sat down on my dining room chairs. I had left my home with nothing but a change of clothes. After I went with my friends to get some more things from our townhouse, I still had very little furniture and no money to buy more. I slept on a mattress on the floor, and I had a table and chairs and a lounger, and that was it.

I was in a one-bedroom apartment in a locked area, and Flo had used all her powers of persuasion and prayers to get past the guard to find me alone in my apartment. Cell phones had yet to be invented. Flo said she just wanted to make sure I was all right and to say that what the Bible study group had done to me was wrong. When I could do nothing at all but stare into space in stunned silence, Flo was my advocate. I understood the reasoning of their decision but not the reaction and the cruelty of it all. This was especially true when the decision came from a person who looked "perfect with a perfect marriage and perfect children" and had the compassion of a gnat. Flo gave me Acts 20:32 (NASB) to read. "And now I commend you to God and the word of His grace, which is able to build you up and to give you the inheritance among all those who are sanctified." What a blessing Flo was!

"But God" is one of my favorite phrases in the Bible. But God met my tears with compassion. But God held my aching body with freedom. But God brought me friends who gave me what I did not know was missing. Songs, sermons, comments were all touched with

God's grace. My lifeline was Jesus as my friend and Savior. He kept me tethered on earth when I wanted to escape to heaven.

But God had heard my cries. A new job in my family's hometown came with double my salary. My husband filed for divorce, and it proceeded with a lessened cost to me. The Bible study leader called and apologized and asked me to stay until spring and teach. I joined a church choir and used my music as a creative outlet. Work at the hospital was successful. I grew the business and had a wonderful boss who was a godly friend. I planned and took the trip to Switzerland in the spring. People acknowledged they knew about my husband's sexual orientation there, but never told me. I knew that the marriage had allowed me to be a "missionary" in a foreign land, and my spiritual children surrounded me with their love. My story was part of God's bigger story, and His love and sacrifices are more real to me now.

Journal

October 31, 1992

The final journal entry

Two years ago today we landed in Chicago O'Hare Airport returning to America after almost three years in Switzerland. Two years, and our worlds are totally changed. I am alone in an apartment surrounded by my things. I have had no personal face-to-face communication with my husband of 12 years in the last three months. After feeling the intense rejection of three days last week, I have had one week of pure joy and acceptance.

I wrote my husband to go ahead and file for divorce. I will sign the waiver.

The head of Bible study called and apologized for the previous decision. If I come back into leadership this week, then my divorce proceedings do not disqualify me for this entire year from teaching or anything. She was grace, strength, relieving of my guilt and shame, and wonderful. I am still mad at God, but it will pass.

Is it a fantasy to be loved? To comfort someone and not be controlled? To support and not smother? To touch gently with no pain? Does Bible study act as my shield for not being in any relationship until next year?

Therapy revealed the reason for the pain. I was stripped to my core by the identities being taken away. Feeling worthless revealed my shame, feeling not good enough to be loved just for me. The feelings included: anger, sadness, fear, and rejection. The pain of knowing that all these identities and my addiction to them must be replaced by the Holy Spirit in order to finally have joy. My assignment seems possible but hard: to read what God says about me and believe it. Daily.

God gives each of us the hardest thing we have to do in a marriage: a wife must respect her husband, and a husband must love his wife as he loves himself. God knew that his human creations would have no problem doing just the opposite but calls us to the difficult task. Women have no problem loving, usually, and men respect their women because of their abilities and what they can give to themselves and others. But ask a woman to respect her man totally, and ask a man to love his wife unconditionally—it is difficult to achieve this without God.

Decades later, I talk publicly and openly about the reason for my divorce. Someone has told me that my Christian ex-husband is living with another man. I did not contract HIV or AIDS nor do I think he had the disease. A woman named Flo would not let a guard keep her away from me as a friend and woman in need. A woman named Renae would not let me be alone during a terrifying, funny, and challenging time. I survived deception and help others in similar circumstances.

I saw the stunned silence of a lady in my Bible study as we talked about how a marriage is supposed to be. After many weeks in the study, she finally acknowledged the years of verbal and emotional abuse from her husband. She expressed her inability to make a change, her shame and fear, not knowing how she would survive financially with no education or job experience, and her worry about how to "get out safely." I stayed after class and spoke with her about her options with domestic abuse, her animals, money, safety, and the lessons she was teaching her children about how to treat and be treated by others. She is a Christian woman who has stayed in this situation over twenty years. She looks to be age fifty, but her true age is closer to forty.

One day, a couple of months after her revelation, she called me and said, "I am leaving him tonight to go to the shelter. Can you take my cat?" One of the reasons people stay in abusive situations is because of the concern they have for the furry members of their families. They know that when the spouse comes home to an empty house—no clothes, no children, no food on the table—they may take their frustration out on the animals. She brought the cat to my house and left for the shelter. Another lady took care of her dog for the two months she was in the shelter.

When the people at the shelter helped her to confront him, set up the separation agreement, and go to the initial meeting with the spouse, she called me again. She was still scared of the future, but being out of the pressure cooker of abuse had literally changed her and her family almost overnight. Later, her husband moved out of the house. The two kids and mom were going back to the house to pack their things to move to a cheaper place. She had a job, and her daughter had a scholarship to college. I went with them to pray, to cleanse the rooms of the evil memories, to help them say goodbye and move on to their new lives.

I counsel young and older women who are in similar situations with a gay or bisexual man. They may have dated or married the man they loved, only to be painfully deceived. The women who have lived this lie for decades are shocked that I am open about the situation, especially in a Christian environment. Shame consumes them because of the failed marriage and if they divorced, because they stayed for so long. The young women question their identity and whether they were active sexually with the bisexual/homosexual man or not. It confronts the core of their femininity and whom God made them.

They question themselves the same way everyone asks me. "How can I not have known?" The answer is not simple. The evil one is a deceiver and a liar, and he enters into human relationships wherever possible. People are broken and have a story that must be healed by Christ Jesus. People hurt other people. There is a reason for your sufferings, and you will use this experience to help others if you choose to heal. Choose healing. Choose hope.

> Lord, put your arms around me.
> Hold me close
> Until Your time is met and I am
> Free to love again.

I took you from the ends of the earth, from its farthest corners I called you. I said, 'You are my servant'; I have chosen you and have not rejected you. So do not fear, for I am with you; do not be dismayed, for I am your God. I will strengthen you and help you; I will uphold you with my righteous right hand. All who rage against you will surely be ashamed and disgraced; those who oppose you will be as nothing and perish. (Isaiah 41:9–11, NIV)

AFTERWORD

What do you do when you suspect or have confirmed that your Christian spouse is gay?

Retreat, seek refuge, and minimize risks to your personal safety. My scariest issue was getting tested for possible exposure to HIV/AIDS. Fortunately for me, I tested negative, and I do not think he tested positive. If you test positive, you face health issues for the rest of your life, even though there are medications available. You need money to survive, and if you have joint accounts, you are entitled to half of the amount during the separation. It is vital in any separation or divorce that you take the steps to cancel joint credit cards, contact your mortgage or rental companies, bank, and your employer (just say you are separating). Notify your children's school if you intend to try to keep your spouse away from the children.

Make a plan to meet the basic needs of shelter, food, transportation, and clothing for you and your children, with or without your spouse. Establish a safe refuge while you process all these changes. Enlist friends with whom you can live, or gather money to cover expenses if you move out on your own.

Reflect on what comments you will answer. What comments will you accept or reject from friends, family, counselors, spouse and church family? People will ask: "Do you have to leave him?" "Are you sure?" "How could you not know?" "Why are you leaving? Him/Her? The Marriage?" "Maybe they will repent or change?" "What will you tell the children?" "Can't you work this out?" "What about his reputation?" "How are you going to tell his family why you are moving out?" "What is God telling you to do?" Your responses will come easier if you plan in advance what you will say. Many people will support and be concerned for both of you. (See Matthew 19:4–6.)

Know the ramifications and consequences to yourself and your spouse. Public exposure of a split in a marriage between Christians when one partner is gay is traumatic. Even today, when it is more common and public figures have been identified as bisexual or gay, do not underestimate how this will affect you at every level.

- Spiritual: You must cling to God's word and prayer to give you answers to this unexpected betrayal as in any separation and divorce. This is adultery of the most challenging kind.
- Emotional: You will feel betrayal, anger, guilt, and shame. You cannot trust your emotions to lead you to good decisions at this time. But your emotions can give you a window to your heart. You may be attracted to other people who affirm your sexuality, and it is a dangerous time for new relationships.
- Physical: The results (positive or negative) for HIV/AIDS or any sexually transmitted disease will impact the rest of your life. Whether it is positive or negative, you may struggle to have energy to exercise, work, or even take care of basic needs.
- Intellectual: You wonder, "How stupid am I? How could I not know? Was he/she laughing at me?"
- Sexual: You rethink every sexual encounter with your spouse, and you remember strange intimacies and encounters. You will wonder what future marital/sexual partner you might have if you divorce. How will you ever trust again? (See Jeremiah 17:7–8.)

Resolve what and how you will communicate. There is a right path for you. Think about this in advance of the situation, be prepared with thoughtfulness, and do not react with pure emotion. Who do you tell, how, and when? Who is safe to communicate with? Who do you think will expose your "shameful" secret to others? What consequences will you face if you are open about why you are leaving? Will he/she sue you for slander? What about their anger regarding the exposure to the church and community? What are your opinions on gay lifestyle? How do you feel when you were betrayed is this manner? What will you say to your pastor, your family, work colleagues, your children, the friend's parents, your "couple" friends, and your personal friends? (See Matthew 5:11–12.)

Recognize the requirement for a community of support. Don't do this alone. You need friends who grieve, socialize, and consistently communicate with you. You need help to move your physical possessions out of the home. You need professional counselors to help you process this change for both you and your children. Your family has lost their son or daughter, and you have lost your spouse's family. Both your families are dealing with this news and grieving the loss of their illusions. The church family support or lack of support may be challenging, especially if the spouse denies the truth of why you left or tells a different story. (See 1 Peter 4:10-11.)

Resolution and conclusions. This "trial" will require earnest seeking of God's will for your life and the consequences of your spouse's choices. You will question everything you ever thought about your relationship. You will grieve the loss of future good times and understand the bad times with greater clarity. You will come to accept the change. Decide if you will separate, stay married, or divorce. The gay spouse is dealing with the same issues, and you may choose not to talk with them about custody and financial issues without counseling and legal support. You will have to deal with the acceptance of their same-sex partner in the future if they choose the gay lifestyle. You will have to tell any children or grandchildren about why you are divorcing, and this will cause them to hear things they would rather not know. You will survive and, with God's help, put together a future. (See 1 Corinthians 6:18–20.)

Is the person you are dating or married to really into you, or are they same-sex attracted?

1. Does he or she notice and comment on people of the opposite sex? Comments about what a person of the same sex is wearing, their attractiveness, or prolonged eye contact is something to watch.
2. Are they homophobic? Do they make disparaging comments about gay people? My gay spouse came to me in a panic because an obviously gay man was following him around a museum. He was fearful and said nasty things about the man. I mistakenly ignored it.
3. Has he or she ever been sexually abused? This is a necessary conversation, but not easy. Knowing who sexually abused them, in what way, and if they received therapy to deal with the abuse is an important clue to their identity and healing. Childhood abuse is a common occurrence. Its impact should not be underestimated and must be acknowledged.
4. Have they shared any sexual fantasies that are disturbing or uncomfortable to you? What do they specifically tell you they want to do? Have this discussion before marriage. Be aware of your reaction to their fantasies. Know your comfort level.
5. Do they hide their internet browser history or phone texts? If you ask to see their phone unexpectedly or if you look at their texts or their computer browsing history, do they freak out or become uncomfortable?
6. If they say you are paranoid or they question whether you trust them, persist in this line of inquiry. Be ready to share your phone and computer as well. Be prepared to deal with what you discover.
7. Have they ever engaged in a same-sex friendship that had a romantic component? Everyone has a story of his or her best friend. Asking whether any of their friends or acquaintances ever approached them romantically is challenging and necessary. Their reaction to those experiences is telling.

8. How old are they? What is their sexual history? How long have they been single? Questions regarding their past and how they have handled normal sexual desires may be revealing for how they will relate to you. If they have never had a relationship with someone of the opposite sex, why? If they have never had sex and choose not to until marriage, then discuss how they have handled their desires. Be prepared to discuss your own history as well.

9. Do they enjoy hugging and kissing you? Even with differing views of Christian boundaries, is there a sexual spark for both of you? Sexual attraction is necessary for a long-term, successful marriage, and physical attraction should be mutual. If you are happy that they are not "pawing" you or trying to go farther, or you tell yourself the attraction will come in the future, be very cautious. This can be a reflection on your sexual history as well, so make sure you are healthy and healed.

10. Are they really sexually attracted to you? Talk about your sexual expectations if you are to marry, including frequency, type, boundaries, and fantasies. Counselors will ask these questions and for good reason: you need to have this discussion before marriage. Things may change, but at least you have discussed expectations and have some level of agreement.

11. Are they obsessed about their appearance, spending time in the gym, shopping for clothes, and personal grooming? Are they attracted to you as you are, right now? Does your dating or marriage partner compliment you or subtly berate you? Do they expect you to look or dress differently than you do right now? Buying you new clothes that they like or enjoying hobbies that are physically active are good things, but if they are trying to change you, be cautious.

Source:
Robert Weiss, Psychology Today 1, 2, 3

ABOUT THE AUTHOR

Debi Nottingham has been writing stories and journaling her own life for decades. She is an avid world traveler and has hiked in all fifty states in the USA. She traveled to China to ride elephants for her sixtieth birthday and rode camels in Egypt for her fiftieth birthday. Debi is an accomplished businesswoman in healthcare marketing and owns an "escape room" business. She is a wife, step-mother, and has five grandchildren. Her education includes a BS in medical technology from Indiana University and an MBA from the University of Houston. She is a university teacher, speaker for Stonecroft Ministries, mentor with 4Word, and a former Bible Study Fellowship Teaching Leader. She is a writer, pianist, artist, entrepreneur, and a teacher who shares her experiences of cancer, infertility, divorce, and hope. Learn more on her blog debdays.wordpress.com.